THE GREEN BOOK OF

SUDOKU
200 PUZZLES

The Puzzle Society™
puzzlesociety.com

**Andrews McMeel
Publishing, LLC**
Kansas City • Sydney • London

Andrews McMeel Publishing, LLC,
an Andrews McMeel Universal company
1130 Walnut Street, Kansas City, Missouri 64106

www.andrewsmcmeel.com

10 11 12 13 RR2 10 9 8 7 6 5 4

ISBN: 978-0-7407-7993-0

www.puzzlesociety.com

Certified Chain of Custody
60% Certified Fiber Sourcing and
40% Post-Consumer Recycled
www.sfiprogram.org

The SFI label only applies to the text stock.

Attention: Schools and Businesses
Andrews McMeel books are available at quantity discounts with bulk purchase for educational, business, or sales promotional use. For information, please e-mail the Andrews McMeel Publishing Special Sales Department: specialsales@amuniversal.com

HOW TO PLAY

Complete the grid so that every row, column, and 3 x 3 cube contains every digit from 1 to 9 inclusive with no repetition.

5	1	8	7	2	4	6	9	3
2	3	6	5	8	9	4	7	1
9	7	4	6	3	1	8	2	5
8	6	7	9	5	2	3	1	4
3	2	9	4	1	6	5	8	7
1	4	5	8	7	3	2	6	9
6	5	1	2	4	7	9	3	8
4	9	3	1	6	8	7	5	2
7	8	2	3	9	5	1	4	6

Difficulty rating:

2

7	4	3	5	9	2	8	6	1
9	8	1	6	7	4	2	5	3
6	2	5	3	8	1	9	4	7
1	7	2	9	5	3	6	8	4
3	6	4	8	2	7	1	9	5
8	5	9	1	4	6	3	7	2
2	9	7	4	1	8	5	3	6
4	3	8	2	6	5	7	1	9
5	1	6	7	3	9	4	2	8

Difficulty rating: 🍃🍃🍃🍃🍃

7	9	8	1	5	3	4	6	2
6	2	5	4	9	7	8	3	1
3	1	4	8	2	6	7	9	5
5	8	9	7	4	2	3	1	6
2	7	3	5	6	1	9	8	4
1	4	6	3	8	9	5	2	7
9	5	7	2	1	8	6	4	3
8	3	1	6	7	4	2	5	9
4	6	2	9	3	5	1	7	8

Difficulty rating: 🌿🌿🌿🌿🌿

4

2	3	8	6	7	4	5	1	9
9	6	4	2	1	5	3	7	8
1	5	7	3	8	9	2	4	6
3	2	1	9	5	7	8	6	4
6	4	9	8	3	2	7	5	1
8	7	5	4	6	1	9	2	3
5	1	3	7	9	6	4	8	2
7	8	2	1	4	3	6	9	5
4	9	6	5	2	8	1	3	7

Difficulty rating: 🌿 🌿 🌿 🌿 🌿

3	6	1	7	4	5	8	2	9
9	7	8	1	2	6	5	3	4
2	4	5	3	9	8	6	7	1
6	1	9	4	7	2	3	8	5
4	8	2	9	5	3	7	1	6
7	5	3	6	8	1	9	4	2
5	2	4	8	3	9	1	6	7
8	9	6	2	1	7	4	5	3
1	3	7	5	6	4	2	9	8

Difficulty rating: 🌿🌿🌿🌿🌿

6

5	6	7	3	8	9	2	4	1
3	1	9	4	6	2	8	7	5
2	8	4	5	1	7	9	6	3
1	3	2	9	4	8	6	5	7
4	5	6	2	7	3	1	9	8
7	9	8	6	5	1	3	2	4
8	7	5	1	2	6	4	3	9
6	4	3	8	9	5	7	1	2
9	2	1	7	3	4	5	8	6

Difficulty rating: 🌿 🌿 🌿 🌿 🌿

6	4	8	1	3	2	9	5	7
1	9	5	8	4	7	6	3	2
2	7	3	6	5	9	8	1	4
5	3	1	7	2	8	4	9	6
7	2	9	4	1	6	5	8	3
4	8	6	3	9	5	2	7	1
3	6	4	5	8	1	7	2	9
9	5	7	2	6	3	1	4	8
8	1	2	9	7	4	3	6	5

Difficulty rating: 🌿🌿🌿🌿🌿

8

1	5	9	6	3	2	4	8	7
8	2	7	1	5	4	3	6	9
3	6	4	8	9	7	5	1	2
7	3	8	4	6	1	2	9	5
9	1	2	7	8	5	6	3	4
6	4	5	3	2	9	8	7	1
2	8	1	5	7	3	9	4	6
4	9	3	2	1	6	7	5	8
5	7	6	9	4	8	1	2	3

Difficulty rating: 🖋🖋🖋🖋🖋

5	4	2	8	7	3	1	9	6
8	9	3	6	5	1	2	7	4
6	7	1	4	9	2	8	3	5
4	1	6	3	8	5	7	2	9
3	8	9	7	2	4	5	6	1
7	2	5	9	1	6	3	4	8
1	5	7	2	6	9	4	8	3
2	6	4	5	3	8	9	1	7
9	3	8	1	4	7	6	5	2

Difficulty rating: 🌿 🌿 🌿 🌿 🌿

10

2	6	5	7	4	9	1	3	8
1	7	9	6	3	8	4	2	5
8	3	4	5	2	1	7	6	9
9	8	3	1	5	2	6	7	4
5	4	6	9	7	3	8	1	2
7	1	2	4	8	6	5	9	3
3	5	1	8	9	7	2	4	6
4	2	7	3	6	5	9	8	1
6	9	8	2	1	4	3	5	7

Difficulty rating: 🌿🌿🌿🌿🌿

7	6	3	8	1	4	9	5	2
8	9	4	3	2	5	6	1	7
5	1	2	6	9	7	8	4	3
6	4	8	7	5	2	3	9	1
2	3	9	1	6	8	5	7	4
1	5	7	4	3	9	2	8	6
9	8	1	2	7	3	4	6	5
3	7	5	9	4	6	1	2	8
4	2	6	5	8	1	7	3	9

Difficulty rating: 🍃🍃🍃🍃🍃

2	3	7	6	5	8	4	1	9
9	4	1	3	2	7	6	8	5
8	5	6	9	4	1	7	3	2
7	9	8	5	3	6	1	2	4
1	2	5	7	8	4	9	6	3
4	6	3	2	1	9	5	7	8
3	7	2	4	6	5	8	9	1
5	8	9	1	7	3	2	4	6
6	1	4	8	9	2	3	5	7

Difficulty rating: 🌿🌿🌿🌿🌿

5	6	4	8	3	7	2	9	1
9	2	7	1	4	5	8	3	6
8	1	3	2	6	9	5	4	7
6	4	1	5	7	8	3	2	9
2	9	5	6	1	3	7	8	4
7	3	8	4	9	2	1	6	5
4	5	6	3	8	1	9	7	2
3	7	2	9	5	6	4	1	8
1	8	9	7	2	4	6	5	3

Difficulty rating:

1	9	7	6	4	8	5	2	3
5	4	3		7	2	8	1	6
8	2	6		1		9	4	7
2	5	1	8	9		3	6	4
7	3	9	1	6	4	2	5	8
6	8	4	2	2	3	7	9	1
3	6	2		5		4	8	9
9	7	5	4	8	6	1	3	2
4	1	8	2	3	9	6	7	5

Difficulty rating: 🍃🍃🍃🍃🍃

6	1	3	8	5	9	2	4	7
9	7	4	2	6	3	8	1	5
2	8	5	1	4	7	3	9	6
4	9	7	3	2	1	6	5	8
8	3	6	9	7	5	1	2	4
5	2	1	4	8	6	9	7	3
7	6	9	5	3	2	4	8	1
3	4	2	7	1	8	5	6	9
1	5	8	6	9	4	7	3	2

Difficulty rating: 🌿 🌿 🌿 🌿 🌿

4	8	5	1	2	7	3	6	9
2	6	7	4	3	9	5	1	8
1	3	9	8	6	5	7	2	4
3	1	2	6	4	8	9	5	7
5	7	6	3	9	2	4	8	1
9	4	8	5	7	1	6	3	2
7	9	1	2	5	3	8	4	6
6	2	3	7	8	4	1	9	5
8	5	4	9	1	6	2	7	3

Difficulty rating:

1	2	3	9	5	4	8	6	7
6	7	8	3	1	2	4	5	9
9	5	4	7	6	8	2	1	3
4	9	6	2	7	5	1	3	8
8	3	2	1	4	6	7	9	5
5	1	7	8	3	9	6	2	4
7	4	9	5	2	1	3	8	6
2	6	5	4	8	3	9	7	1
3	8	1	6	9	7	5	4	2

Difficulty rating: 🍃🍃🍃🍃🍃

18

9	3	1	4	5	6	2	7	8
5	4	8	3	7	2	1	9	6
2	7	6	9	1	8	4	5	3
3	6	4	8	9	1	7	2	5
7	9	2	6	3	5	8	4	1
8	1	5	2	4	7	6	3	9
6	8	3	7	2	9	5	1	4
1	2	9	5	8	4	3	6	7
4	5	7	1	6	3	9	8	2

Difficulty rating: 🌿 🌿 🌿 🌿 🌿

9	5	6	4	7	8	1	2	3
1	8	7	6	3	2	5	4	9
3	2		5	1	9	7	6	8
8	3	2	9	5	4	6	7	1
6	7	1	2	8	3	4	9	5
5	4	9	7	6	1	3	8	2
7	9	3	8	4	5	2	1	6
4	1	8	3	2	6	9	5	7
2	6	5	1	9	7	8	3	4

Difficulty rating:

2	6	9	8	5	4	3	1	7
1	4	5	3	9	7	8	6	2
3	8	7	2	6	1	9	5	4
6	2	1	9	7	3	5	4	8
5	7	3	4	8	2	6	9	1
8	9	4	5	1	6	7	2	3
9	5	2	1	3	8	4	7	6
7	1	8	6	4	9	2	3	5
4	3	6	7	2	5	1	8	9

Difficulty rating: 🖋🖋🖋🖋🖋

2	1	6	9	5	3	4	8	7
4	3	5	8	7	6	1	2	9
8	9	7	4	2	1	5	3	6
9	8	1	5	6	7	2	4	3
6	2	4	3	1	8	9	7	5
7	5	3	2	9	4	8	6	1
3	6	9	1	4	2	7	5	8
1	7	2	6	8	5	3	9	4
5	4	8	7	3	9	6	1	2

Difficulty rating: 🌿 🌿 🌿 🌿 🌿

1	4	6	3	5	7	9	8	2
7	5	2	6	9	8	1	3	4
8	9	3	2	1	4	7	6	5
6	7	5	9	8	2	3	4	1
4	3	9	1	7	6	5	2	8
2	1	8	4	3	5	6	7	9
5	6	7	8	4	9	2	1	3
3	2	4	5	6	1	8	9	7
9	8	1	7	2	3	4	5	6

Difficulty rating: 🌿 🌿 🌿 🌿 🌿

7	5	1	9	3	4	2	6	8
6	9	4	8	2	7	5	1	3
2	3	8	5	1	6	9	7	4
9	7	5	1	4	2	8	3	6
3	4	2	7	6	8	1	5	9
8	1	6	3	9	5	7	4	2
4	2	7	6	8	1	3	9	5
1	6	9	2	5	3	4	8	7
5	8	3	4	7	9	6	2	1

Difficulty rating: 🍃 🍃 🍃 🍃 🍃

5		3		8		2	6	1
		2			5			9
	2	9	6	1	7			5
	4	8				7	1	
7	1			9			5	3
	5	6	1			4	9	
6			7	2	1	9	3	
4		1	9					
2	9			4		1		6

Difficulty rating: 🍃🍃🍃🍃🍃

6	2	4	9	7				3
		3		1		2		
1				2		5		
	4			3	6		2	5
2	3	1		9		4	6	8
8	5		2	4			9	
		5		6				2
				5	2	9		
7		2		8	9	6	5	4

Difficulty rating: 🍃 🍃 🍃 🍃 🍃

8			1	2		3		4
1	7			3		9	8	
	3			8			2	1
	4	1	2				3	
7			4	6	9			8
	6				1	4	7	
4	8			9			1	
	1	7		4			9	6
3		5		1	6			7

Difficulty rating: 🌿🌿🌿🌿🌿

5	2			4		6		
7		9	2	3	6		1	
	3		9	5		2	4	
3	6	7				4		8
				8				
8		2				7	5	9
	5	6		7	4		3	
	8		6	2	5	1		4
		4		1			8	6

Difficulty rating: 🌿🌿🌿🌿🌿

4			6		5	7		8
		5		1	7		2	6
	1	7		8	2	4		5
	4					5	6	
9				5				4
	8	6					7	
7		8	3	6		1	4	
1	2		7	4		6		
3		4	5		1			7

Difficulty rating: 🍃🍃🍃🍃🍃

			2	9			1	
5					8	3	6	7
1	8	4		7	3	2		
	1	8			9			2
	9			5			3	
2			1			6	8	
		1	3	2		9	5	6
9	3	7	5					4
	5			4	1			

Difficulty rating:

30

	6	8	3				2	
		2		6		9	3	
5				9	2			6
4	9	6	8	2		7		
	8	1		7		6	4	
		5		1	6	3	9	8
6			2	8				5
	2	7		5		4		
	5				7	2	6	

Difficulty rating: 🍃 🍃 🍃 🍃 🍃

	8		6		2		1	
2					3		5	
6	1		8	5		2		4
3	7		9	8	6			2
8				7				3
9			5	3	4		8	1
4		8		9	7		2	5
	9		4					7
	2		3		5		9	

Difficulty rating:

		4		1	5			
1	9	2		7		4		5
7		5		9	4		8	
2				5	1			
5		3		2		8		6
			6	8				1
	5		9	6		3		8
3		8		4		6	1	9
			1	3		2		

Difficulty rating: 🖋 🖋 🖋 🖋 🖋

		3	7	6		2		8
	6	7	2	9	8		3	
2					4		7	6
				2				3
4		8	9		6	7		5
7			5					
8	1		6					2
	5		1	8	9	6	4	
9		6		2	5	3		

Difficulty rating:

6		4			8	9	2	7
8	7	5	4	9	2			1
9			6					
				6	5			4
3	1						8	6
5			1	8				
					6			3
7			2	5	1	8	4	9
1	9	2	8			7		5

Difficulty rating: 🍃 🍃 🍃 🍃 🍃

6	5	7		8	1			9
4	2			9	3	8	7	
			2					1
7	4	5	8					2
2								4
1					2	7	9	5
5					8			
	3	2	7	6			1	8
8			3	2		9	5	7

Difficulty rating: 🌿🌿🌿🌿🌿

	3	5						
		8	9	4	7	1		3
		1		3		8	2	4
	9	4		5	2			8
5		2		6		9		1
3			4	9		5	6	
8	2	3		7		4		
1		9	2	8	6	7		
						2	8	

Difficulty rating: 🖋

9				8			1	6
	3			5	1			
5	6		7			3		2
		9		4			3	5
6		3	5		7	2		4
4	5			3		8		
1		4			3		5	7
			1	2			6	
8	9			7				3

Difficulty rating: 🍃 🍃 🍃 🍃 🍃

38

2	5		9	8				
9		8		3	6			
3		1		4	5		9	
	2	9		7			1	4
	7	4	8		2	3	6	
5	3			1		2	8	
	8		5	6		9		1
			3	9		4		6
				2	4		7	5

Difficulty rating: 🖋 🖋 🖋 🖋 🖋

8		9	1	3	7	2		
2		1		4		9		
4	7		9	8				
				1	4		9	3
9				2				4
5	8		7	9				
				5	1		7	9
		2		7		5		8
		5	4	6	8	3		1

Difficulty rating:

9	4			2	3			8
8				4		2	3	5
	7			8		1	4	
7				1	9	8		6
	1			7			5	
2		9	4	6				3
	9	7		3			6	
5	2	3		9				1
4			2	5			9	7

Difficulty rating: 🪶 🪶 🪶 🪶 🪶

	8	4		3	5			6
		2		7	6		8	4
6				1			2	3
5	6			4			1	2
		7		8		3		
8	4			2			7	9
4	3			5				7
7	1		3	9		2		
2			8	6		4	3	

Difficulty rating:

42

6	5	3	7	2	4	8		9
	7	8	5	1			4	6
				6				
	2		9					1
	6			5			9	
4					1		2	
				8				
5	4			7	3	9	6	
8		6	4	9	5	2	3	7

Difficulty rating: 🌿🌿🌿🌿🌿

	7		2		6	8	4	
8				1	4	7		
	4			8			3	2
3	6	1		4				8
	8		1	7	9		6	
5				3		4	2	1
7	3			2			9	
		8	4	6				7
	1	2	7		5		8	

Difficulty rating: 🌿 🌿 🌿 🌿 🌿

44

2	8		7	3				
	5	4	9	8		6	3	
		7		4	1			
	9	1		7		3		8
	3	2				9	7	
4		8		6		2	1	
			8	5		7		
	2	5		9	7	4	6	
				2	4		8	9

Difficulty rating: 🍃🍃🍃🍃🍃

7	1		5		6		9	
8	2		3			5		6
				8		3	7	
	6	9	8	1				7
4				3				1
5				7	4	9	2	
	3	5		6				
1		7			3		6	2
	4		7		9		3	5

Difficulty rating:

46

6	7		5	3				4
	3	4	7					
8		9	4	2		3	7	
	5			8	4			9
9		6		5		8		2
2			1	6			5	
	9	8		4	5	7		3
					2	5	4	
4				7	3		6	1

Difficulty rating: 🍃 🍃 🍃 🍃 🍃

9	6				1			8	
1	2		8	9	7				5
3			5	4			1	9	
8		2	9		4				
		9		3			4		
			2		5		8		9
	9	8		5	1				6
5			4	8	9			7	1
	7			2				5	8

Difficulty rating: 🌿 🌿 🌿 🌿 🌿

		3	1	7		8		9
4				5			6	7
		8	6	3	9			
2		6				1	7	
1	3		4	2	5		9	8
	9	4				2		3
			3	1	7	9		
9	8			4				6
3		5		9	6	4		

Difficulty rating: 🍃 🍃 🍃 🍃 🍃

9			1		3	7	4		
			4		6				
7			2		5	8	6		9
1			7		4			9	
3	8				2			4	6
	4				1		7		2
2			3	5	7		8		4
					9		2		
			5	6	8		9		1

Difficulty rating:

50

1				5	8		3	6
8			9	6	4		1	2
5	6	2		7				
		3			5		2	
6			1	2	3			5
	2		6			3		
				4		1	5	3
3	9		5	1	6			8
7	5		8	3				4

Difficulty rating:

	5	4		2	6	7		9
				1	7		4	5
			4			2		6
7		3		4	5		8	2
		1		8		3		
2	8		7	9		4		1
9		2			4			
6	4		2	7				
5		7	8	3		6	2	

Difficulty rating:

7		8		1	6			
	6		7	3		1	9	8
			9	5	8			6
	2	7			4		3	
9				7				2
	5		8			7	1	
2			6	4	1			
4	1	9		8	5		6	
			2	9		3		1

Difficulty rating: 🍃 🍃 🍃 🍃 🍃

1		7	8	3		4	9	
		3		2		7		
9	4			7	1	5		
6						1	7	5
	5		9	8	7		4	
4	7	2						9
		6	7	1			5	4
		4		6		9		
	1	5		9	4	3		8

Difficulty rating: 🌿 🌿 🌿 🌿 🌿

1		7	6	5			9	
		3			8			1
		6		1	9	7		8
	1	8		6				3
	2	4	1	8	3	5	6	
3				9		1	8	
5		9	8	4		2		
6			9			8		
	4			2	7	9		6

Difficulty rating: 🌿 🌿 🌿 🌿 🌿

8	1	3		4				
	5	7		8	3			1
2			1	7		5	8	
			3	2	4	6		
5								8
		6	8	5	7			
	3	8		9	5			2
4			7	3		8	1	
				1		3	9	4

Difficulty rating:

			2		3	5		6
5	6		9	8				7
1		7		5		9	8	3
	8			1	4			
9	4			2			3	1
			8	9			4	
6	5	2		3		1		4
7				4	2		6	8
8		4	1		9			

Difficulty rating: 🌿🌿🌿🌿🌿

			9	2	7	4	3	
	9		8	3	4			
	4	3			5		9	2
	8	6		9		1	5	
		2	3		1	9		
	1	9		4		2	8	
9	2		4			8	7	
			2	7	9		6	
	7	4	1	5	8			

Difficulty rating:

58

	9		5	7	4			2
3		7	9	8		1	4	
	2			3	1			9
7							9	
	8		4	1	6		2	
	4							3
8			7	4			5	
	5	4		2	3	9		8
2			8	6	5		3	

Difficulty rating:

			3	4	5	6		8
4	6		7		8			3
	3	5		6				2
		4				9	3	1
	8		4		2		6	
5	7	9				2		
7				1		8	4	
9			8		4		2	7
3		8	2	7	6			

Difficulty rating:

4	7			5			1	6
9		6	7	3	4			
2		5	6	1				
	5			4				8
	4	9		8		6	3	
6				7			5	
				6	3	8		7
			8	2	7	5		9
8	2			9			6	1

Difficulty rating: 🌿🌿🌿🌿🌿

		7	6		4	5	3	8
3		2		1		4		
8					5			
4	8			6	3		2	7
5				9				4
2	7		8	4			5	3
			3					5
		5		7		8		6
7	9	8	1		6	3		

Difficulty rating:

62

8					5		7		
6					8		1	2	3
		4	9	1			5	6	8
	2	8				3	6		9
9		6	1				8	4	
4	6	5			3	1	9		
2	9	3			7				1
		1			9				6

Difficulty rating: 🪶🪶🪶🪶🪶

		7	9	2	3			6
6		4		8	1		3	2
3	5			6			9	
9		6		7			1	
				3				
	4			1		8		5
	6			9			5	3
4	3		8	5		6		9
5			3	4	6	2		

Difficulty rating:

2			7		1			6
	7		4	5	3	1		
	3			6		5	8	7
	8			4	7		9	
	1	2		3		8	7	
	4		2	9			1	
1	9	4		7			5	
		3	8	2	9		4	
8			5		4			3

Difficulty rating:

1					9		3	6
	4		3	1		9		5
9			5	8	6	1	4	
8		1		7				
5		6		2		3		1
				6		8		9
	6	9	4	3	1			8
7		3		5	8		9	
4	5		2					3

Difficulty rating:

1		5		8			3	4
	2				4	6		8
	4	6		3	9	5		1
	6		2	9		8		
9				5				2
		7		6	1		4	
6		2	9	7		4	1	
7		8	3				9	
5	9			2		7		3

Difficulty rating: 🍃🍃🍃🍃🍃

9		8			5		7	
5	7		6		8			9
4				9	2		8	3
8	4			1			5	2
		1		2		7		
2	6			8			9	1
6	3		2	5				7
1			8		9		3	6
	8		4			9		5

Difficulty rating:

				2	6			3
7	8	4	1		3	2	5	
2	6	3		8	5		1	
	7				4			2
9				6				4
8			5				9	
	1		2	5		7	4	9
	2	8	3		9	1	6	5
5			6	4				

Difficulty rating: 🌿 🌿 🌿 🌿 🌿

		9			4	8	6	5
5	8			3			9	4
		2		9	8	1		
	2	8	3					9
		4	2	5	1	6		
6					9	3	1	
		3	7	4		9		
7	9			1			4	3
8	4	5	9			7		

Difficulty rating: 🍃 🍃 🍃 🍃 🍃

		6		8	2	5		
7	8		6		5			3
	4		7	9		6	8	2
	9	4		5			6	
			8	3	4			
	2			6		4	3	
2	6	5		7	8		9	
4			3		6		5	8
		3	5	4		2		

Difficulty rating: 🌿 🌿 🌿 🌿 🌿

8	5		4	1	9	2	7	3
7	1	4	2	3	6	5	8	
2		6	7	8	5	1		
5	7	8	1	4	3	9	6	2
1	4	9	5	6	2	8	3	7
6	3	2	9	7	8	4	5	1
						3		5
	6	5	3	9		7		
				5	7	6	9	

Difficulty rating:

	2			9				7
			4	7				8
				3	5	2		4
	5					8	2	1
8		6	7	2	4	5		9
2	9	3					4	
1		2	6	5				
3				8	7			
7				4			8	

Difficulty rating: 🌿🌿🌿🌿🌿

	2	5			6			
4				3	8	2	6	
		3			2		1	4
5				9		8		1
			8		7			
6		9		2				7
2	4		3			5		
	3	8	5	6				2
			2			1	8	

Difficulty rating: 🌿🌿🌿🌿🌿

				8		3	2	
	9			3	4	6	7	
	3			2		9		
9		6			1			2
				4				
5			3			4		6
		9		1			4	
	8	2	4	6			1	
	7	1		9				

Difficulty rating: 🍃🍃🍃🍃🍃

			6		2			3
9			8	7		5		
2						6	1	
				8	5	1		4
	9	8		2		3	5	
5		6	7	4				
	8	4						1
		7		3	9			6
6			4		8			

Difficulty rating:

	6			3	2	8	4	
		2	6	9		3		
			8		5			9
3		4		8				
	5	7		2		4	9	
				5		7		1
8			5		9			
		5		6	1	9		
	4	1	2	7			6	

Difficulty rating: 🍂🍂🍂🍂🍂

9	2	6			7	8			4
7			2	3			1	6	
			5						
		5	3					9	
3									5
	8				1	2			
			1						
	7	9		8	3				2
1			9	2			6	4	7

Difficulty rating:

	8				5	3	6	2
1	6			4	2			
				7			8	
7					9	4		
2	1			8			5	7
		5	7					9
	9			2				
			9	3			2	1
3	2	8	4				9	

Difficulty rating: 🌿🌿🌿🌿🌿

			9					5
				8	6		7	
	6	8	3	5			2	
	7	9			1		3	8
6			7	4	9			1
1	5		8			7	9	
	1			3	4	5	8	
	4		2	9				
8					5			

Difficulty rating: 🌿🌿🌿🌿🌿

80

		3			2			8
	4		8	9	1			7
7	2		3	6				
		4	6	8			9	
		1				8		
	9			4	7	2		
				1	5		8	3
1			9	3	8		6	
3			4			5		

Difficulty rating: 🌿🌿🌿🌿🌿

	1	9		4	3			
		8		7		4		3
		4		6				
		5		3	8			2
8		7		2		6		5
4			6	9		7		
				8		1		
7		3		1		8		
			4	5		3	9	

Difficulty rating: 🍃🍃🍃🍃🍃

4				2	9	5		
9		1	3					
		3		5	7		4	1
8	9			7				
5		2		8		1		9
				6			2	4
6	3		7	1		2		
					6	4		3
		9	5	3				7

Difficulty rating: 🍃🍃🍃🍃🍃

9	6	2		1				
4		8	2	5		6	9	
				6		8	2	
1						7		
7			1	2	8			9
		9						6
	7	4		8				
	9	5		3	6	1		8
				7		9	4	3

Difficulty rating:

		6		8		7	5	
	9			6	5			
8		5	3				4	2
4				7	8	5		
		1				4		
		9	4	2				3
5	1				2	3		4
			8	4			1	
	4	7		3		2		

Difficulty rating:

	5				1	8	3	
			4	5	8	1	7	
		7		2		4		
	9			3		5		
		4		9		3		
		6		7			9	
		9		8		6		
7	1	5	4	3				
8	5	9					4	

Difficulty rating:

	9				2	3		5
5				8		1		
3	1			7			2	
				9	7	8	6	
	6	9	2	5				
	5			2			4	6
		4		3				8
6		7	5				9	

Difficulty rating: 🌿🌿🌿🌿🌿

		9		2				8
	6	2	9	4				
5				8	3		9	
2			3	5			1	
		1		9		8		
	9			1	2			3
	4		2	6				5
				3	5	7	2	
6				7		4		

Difficulty rating:

	4				5		1	2
	6	2			9		8	
5				8		4		6
		8		6				1
7			9	1	3			8
6				2		3		
2		5		9				4
	1		7			2	3	
4	7		1				6	

Difficulty rating:

3	8			9	7			
		9	5			8		2
4				3	1			
2			6	1			9	
6		1				4		7
	3			7	5			1
			9	6				8
8		2			3	9		
			1	8			2	5

Difficulty rating:

9		7			4			8
				7			1	
8			5	6	3		7	9
5						4		3
			2	4	5			
2		1						5
1	9		8	5	7			2
	2			3				
3			4			8		6

Difficulty rating: 🖋🖋 🖋 🖋 🖋

	6			1				
				8	5	4	6	
	3	2		4	7			1
	8	7	1	3		9		
		3		5		1		
		4		9	6	3	8	
3			5	7		6	1	
	1	9	4	6				
				2			5	

Difficulty rating: 🍂🍂🍂🍂🍂

	4	3	6	1	7	8		
				3			6	
					4	7		
	5	1					7	8
	3	8				1	9	
2	7					3	5	
		9	7					
	6			2				
		5	4	6	9	2	1	

Difficulty rating: 🌿🌿🌿🌿🌿

7				3	6			4
		5		7			1	
	6			8	9			
2			6	4		1		
8	3			5			4	2
		1		2	7			5
			3	1			5	
	8			9		3		
9			2	6				8

Difficulty rating: 🌿🌿🌿🌿🌿

94

4	2			7	8	3		
					6		9	7
	3	7	9	1				
5						2	1	
1				2				9
	9	2						3
				4	2	1	3	
3	6		1					
		8	3	6			7	4

Difficulty rating: 🍃🍃🍃🍃🍃

6		3		2		8	9	
2		7		4				1
				3	8	2	5	
		5						
8	9			7			1	6
					9			
	4	8	7	5				
7				6		5		9
	6	1		8		4		2

Difficulty rating:

5				3			9	
	1			6		7		
	6		2	7	1	4	5	3
		7				1		9
			4	1	7			
1		6				5		
6	7	5	1	9	2		8	
		1		5			7	
	2			4			1	

Difficulty rating: 🖊️🖊️🖊️🖊️🖊️

7					1			
	9		3	6	5			
2				9	7	4	5	
6	2						3	
	7	1	6		4	5	8	
	3						7	4
	4	2	7	8				5
			1	5	6		4	
			4					3

Difficulty rating:

7			4	9				6
				8		3	1	
				1		9	5	
6		4						3
	2	1		6		7	4	
5						1		2
	5	6		2				
	8	7		3				
9				7	5			8

Difficulty rating: 🖋🖋🖋🖋🖋

	8			5	4			
5				9	6			7
6	2		7		8		5	
				6	3		2	8
		5				3		
7	3		1	4				
	7		6		1		9	5
9			8	2				4
			4	7			3	

Difficulty rating: 🌿🌿🌿🌿🌿

100

				8		2	6	
2	7			5		8	4	
8			9	2				
5		8		3	2			7
3			4	9		1		8
				7	3			4
	3	2		4			1	5
	8	7		1				

Difficulty rating:

	2		1	8	9			
9	5			6				8
	6				7		4	
2	4					7	8	9
7				2				6
3	8	5					1	4
	9		7				6	
8				4			9	2
			8	9	1		7	

Difficulty rating: 🌿🌿🌿🌿🌿

102

9	8				3		5	6
				4				7
	3		9	5			4	2
2				3			7	
			2	1	5			
	6			7				9
8	2			6	4		1	
4				9				
6	1		3				9	4

Difficulty rating: 🍃🍃🍃🍃🍃

			3	9				7
		7		4	5			1
5	3			1	7			2
	7			6	3			5
3		5	8		1	7		9
2			5	7			8	
4			1	5			7	3
1			7	8		5		
7				3	2			

Difficulty rating: 🌿🌿🌿🌿🌿

104

				3		2		8
	4					6	5	
	6	7	9			1		3
1	3			6			2	
		2		4		5		
	9			7			6	4
4		6			3	8	9	
	2	3					1	
5		9		1				

Difficulty rating: 🪶🪶🪶🪶🪶

			5	8	1	3	2	
5	2			3		1	8	
				2			4	
6	5		1			2		
	4			7			9	
		7			3		1	6
	6			1				
	9	1		5			6	8
	3	4	8	6	9			

Difficulty rating: 🍃🍃🍃🍃🍃

3		4		1				
			6	9		1		4
1			7		4			2
	1	5		6		3		
	3			4			7	
		7		8		2	1	
9			4		6			3
6		3		5	9			
				7		6		9

Difficulty rating: 🌿🌿🌿🌿🌿

				3	5			9
	3	9	6		1			
2	1	4	7	9		6		
	5	7		2				
9			4	5	7			3
				1		5	7	
		3		7	2	1	4	8
			1		3	9	5	
1			9	8				

Difficulty rating: 🌿🌿🌿🌿🌿

108

5			8	4	9	6	2	
		6						3
7		9		3	2		5	
		7			1			6
	5			8			4	
9			3			7		
	9		2	5		8		1
3						5		
	1	5	4	6	3			9

Difficulty rating: 🍃🍃🍃🍃🍃

				7				4
		8	2	5	9			3
9	6		1				8	
	8		4					5
	9			6			2	
7					2		1	
	1				3		4	6
8			9	2	6	5		
3				4				

Difficulty rating: 🌿🌿🌿🌿🌿

110

				4		2		
2	1	8		7		3		4
		3		1	8		7	
8				3		6		
	6	9		5		1	2	
		4		6				8
	3		7	8		4		
6		5		2		7	9	3
		7		9				

Difficulty rating: 🌿🌿🌿🌿🌿

4			3		5		2	
	5		6		2	9	4	3
3				4		6		
		3		6				
6			9	3	1			7
				2		3		
		9		5				2
2	3	6	4		9		5	
	1		2		3			9

Difficulty rating:

112

	9			4	3	6		
2	4		1	6	7			3
			5				1	
			7			9	3	4
	5			3			2	
4	3	9			6			
	8				5			
5			6	7	9		4	8
		7	4	8			6	

Difficulty rating: 🌿🌿🌿🌿🌿

		1		9	4			
3	4			5	7		2	
	7	2	1			9		8
6				2				7
4		3			9	2	6	
	6		7	3			4	2
			9	1		3		

Difficulty rating: 🌿🌿🌿🌿🌿

114

1				6	3			
				1	7	8		6
		8	5				7	4
		6		5		9		8
				2				
7		5		8		2		
2	6				5	4		
5		1	6	4				
			2	7				9

Difficulty rating: 🌿🌿🌿🌿🌿

	3		7		8			
5				9		2		
	1	8		2	4			
						5		
1	9	3		6		4	7	8
		5						
			1	7		3	9	
		2		8				7
			9		6		2	

Difficulty rating: 🌿🌿🌿🌿🌿

			8	4				2
			6	1		5		4
4	5			7				6
		9		8			3	
	4		2	5	3		9	
	7			9		8		
7				2			6	3
3		4		6	1			
1				3	8			

Difficulty rating: 🌿🌿🌿🌿🌿

	4			6				
			2	3		1		7
		1		4	8			3
				2	6	5		
	2			1			6	
		9	5	7				
1			7	9		8		
6		7		5	2			
				8			7	

Difficulty rating: 🌿🌿🌿🌿🌿

					7		5	3
		5	8	6	3			2
	7	8					9	
	8						2	
			7	2	1			
	2						6	
	5					6	1	
7			1	8	5	3		
9	3		4					

Difficulty rating: 🌿🌿🌿🌿🌿

	9	8		7			4	
7	1			9			6	
					2			
5	8			6		2		
		3		4		7		
		4		5			8	9
			6					
	4			3			7	5
	6			2		4	3	

Difficulty rating:

120

				2	6	9		
		9		3		7		
1			9	5	4		8	
							2	6
3	2			6			9	8
8	1							
	6		3	8	1			4
		1		7		8		
		8	4	9				

Difficulty rating: 🌿🌿🌿🌿🌿

	9	8			1	5		
1	7	3		4				
				8	2			
9					8	2		
	4	6		7		9	1	
		1	4					6
			3	1				
				5		3	8	9
		4	8			6	7	

Difficulty rating: 🌿🌿🌿🌿🌿

		6	4	1	2			8
		1		5	3			
	5							
4			1		6	2	9	
6			3		7			1
	2	7	5		4			6
							1	
			2	3		8		
3			8	7	5	9		

Difficulty rating: 🌿🌿🌿🌿🌿

	6			3		8		
2	5	3	9	7			6	
1				4		5		
4					7		8	
		2		1		3		
	3		4					7
		5		9				6
	2			8	4	9	3	1
		1		6			5	

Difficulty rating: 🌿🌿🌿🌿🌿

		6		3				
5			8	6			4	
9				4	7			
3		2		5		9		
		9	6	2	1	7		
		7		9		5		2
			5	8				6
	6			7	4			9
				1		8		

Difficulty rating: 🌿🌿🌿🌿🌿

2			8		5			4
				7			2	
		8		2	4		7	
					2	5		8
	3	7		4		2	6	
5		1	6					
	8		1	3		6		
	4			5				
7			4		8			3

Difficulty rating: 🌿🌿🌿🌿🌿

6	9			1				
		8		7	6			5
7			4		1			
		4					2	3
	4		6		8			
8	1			5				
	6		2					9
5	9	7		6				
			5			6	8	

Difficulty rating: 🖊🖊🖊🖊🖊

								1
	9		5	2				4
				8	1	2		7
	1	3		6		5		
			3	4	8			
		2		7		3	9	
9		5	8	1				
3				9	4		2	
6								

Difficulty rating: ✿✿✿✿✿

128

		3	9	7				
	4			6				3
	9			1		2	5	
4	5			9	2	3		6
				4				
2		9	3	8			4	5
	1	6		2			3	
9				5			7	
				3	4	6		

Difficulty rating: 🌿🌿🌿🌿🌿

7			3	5				
	1		8	7			9	4
	3		1	2			8	
		1		3				5
		4		1		6		
8				4		7		
	4			9	5		7	
9	5			8	1		6	
				6	3			9

Difficulty rating: 🍃🍃🍃🍃🍃

3	1				8		2	7
					3	8		
				1	5			3
		3		2	1		5	8
7		2		5		9		1
5	6		3	8		2		
2			1	9				
		6	5					
1	5		8				6	9

Difficulty rating: 𝒪 𝒪 𝒪 𝒪 𝒪

			5	8				7
	6	8		3	7	2		
5				9				
	3	4	2	1	9			
7				5				8
			8	7	6	9	4	
				2				9
		3	9	6		4	7	
9				4	5			

Difficulty rating:

132

		8	2	9				3
				1	4			
2					8	6		9
		3		2				
8	1		6	4	5		3	2
				7		1		
1		7	9					5
			5	3				
9				6	7	2		

Difficulty rating: 🌿🌿🌿🌿🌿

			7	9	4	3		
			8					6
3		4		2			1	
					9			7
	9			8			5	
2			1					
	3			1		6		5
8					5			
		5	2	6	7			

Difficulty rating: 🌿🌿🌿🌿🌿

				1	8	5	7	
				6				
4		2		3	7	6	8	9
		5		4	9		2	
7				2				5
	2		3	5		8		
9	8	6	4	7		2		1
				8				
	5	7	1	9				

Difficulty rating: 🌿🌿🌿🌿🌿

		7					4	
	8	3	5	1	6			
				9	4	3	1	
			3	4		8		
8								3
		6		7	9			
	9	5	4	2				
			1	8	3	9	5	
	2					4		

Difficulty rating: 🌿🌿🌿🌿🌿

	8		1	7			3	
				6	9	4		
	7			2	3			
8				3		6	7	
1								3
	9	5		8				2
			2	1			9	
		1	3	9				
	3			4	7		1	

Difficulty rating: 🌿🌿🌿🌿🌿

	3	2					1	
	6	4	1	9				
				6				8
	5		3	1		9		
		3		7		1		
		9		4	5		2	
7				3				
			2	4		8	6	
	8					2	3	

Difficulty rating: 🌿🌿🌿🌿🌿

138

6			3	2		9		
	3			1			5	6
				5	9	3		
		2		4		8		
	9		2		1		3	
		3		9		1		
		9	1	7				
8	1			6			4	
		7		3	5			1

Difficulty rating: 🌿🌿🌿🌿🌿

2			7		9			
	7			1			3	6
		6		3		9		
7	1		3				4	
	9			4			6	
	6				5		2	1
		1		8		4		
4	8			9			5	
			4		1			3

Difficulty rating: 🌿🌿🌿🌿🌿

		3	4	6		9		8
		7		1				
		4		5	2			
	7							2
	1		5	8	4		9	
3							5	
			7	4		8		
				9		2		
8		6		2	3	7		

Difficulty rating: 🌿🌿🌿🌿🌿

			6		1		4	
				2			7	
				4		3	2	
	8	5			9			3
1			2		3			4
3			5			6	9	
	7	8		3				
	9			8				
	3		9		2			

Difficulty rating:

142

				4	6		5	
	4			1	7			3
	9	7		2				
	5	6	4					1
			1	6	3			
8					2	6	3	
				3		7	8	
5			7	9			1	
	7		6	5				

Difficulty rating: 🌿🌿🌿🌿🌿

1		7		9	6	2	8	
				3				5
		7	2		3			
		1	2		5			7
		3		1		6		
4			3		8	1		
		5		7	3			
3				8				
	8	9	6	5		4		3

Difficulty rating: 🌿🌿🌿🌿🌿

	3	6		4				
2				5			6	
	1		3	9	6			
8		4		2	1			6
	7	2		3		9	1	
1			6	8		4		2
			8	1	3		2	
	2			7				1
				6		3	9	

Difficulty rating: 🌿🌿🌿🌿🌿

				1	6		2	
		2	5		8	9		3
							1	5
		6		3		8		
5								9
		8		9		2		
2	8							
6		7	9		3	1		
	3		1	7				

Difficulty rating: 🌿🌿🌿

146

		8		6	9			
2				3	5	7		
4	5	6	8					
6		9						7
	7			5			9	
3						4		6
					4	8	3	2
		2	3	8				9
			9	2		5		

Difficulty rating: 🌿🌿🌿🌿🌿

	8	1	5	9		4	3	
9				4				
7	5			1				8
	6		7				8	5
		8		6		7		
2	7				4		6	
1				7			5	2
				5				3
	2	7		3	6	8	4	

Difficulty rating: 🌿🌿🌿🌿🌿

		8		3	9	1		
		5	2	1				6
				5			9	
	9				5		1	
				2				
	3		6				7	
	2			8				
4				7	1	2		
		1	5	6		3		

Difficulty rating: 🌿🌿🌿🌿🌿

				3				6
	9	3		1	6			4
6			7	9		3	5	
					4	1		
8				6				9
		7	8					
	1	9		5	7			8
7			9	4		5	3	
3				8				

Difficulty rating: 🌿🌿🌿🌿🌿

150

		3		2	9	4		
		2	1		6		3	
7							1	
		5	8					1
1		4		6		8		3
8					1	5		
	2							4
	5		6		7	1		
		1	4	5		6		

Difficulty rating: 🌿🌿🌿🌿🌿

9				3	5		2	
	1			2	9			
				8		1		
1		7		5		6	4	
				6				
	4	3		1		8		2
		9		4				
			3	9			8	
	2		6	7				3

Difficulty rating: 🍃🍃🍃🍃🍃

152

8					7			1
2		4			6	7		
	1		8	4	2			5
	2					8		
9				1				7
		6					3	
3			5	6	9		1	
		5	2			3		6
6			7					8

Difficulty rating: 🍃🍃🍃🍃🍃

	7				4			
				5	9		2	7
5		3	6					
4		8		1		5	7	
		5				8		
	3	7		4		2		1
					7	1		6
3	1		9	6				
			4				9	

Difficulty rating: 🍃🍃🍃🍃🍃

154

		4				8		
7				9	8			
6	2			3	1			9
4		7		5	9			
			3		6			
			8	4		5		2
5			6	7			4	1
			1	8				5
		6				3		

Difficulty rating: 🍃🍃🍃🍃🍃

					1		5	
				9		3	4	
	2		3	6				1
	4	3		1			2	7
	8			5			3	
5	7			4		8	1	
4				2	6		9	
	6	2		3				
	5		8					

Difficulty rating: 🍃🍃🍃🍃🍃

				4		3		
3	4		5	1	6	7		
6		8						
	8	3	1	5			4	
	5						3	
	2			3	4	5	8	
						8		3
		5	3	8	9		6	1
		1		6				

Difficulty rating: 𝄞 𝄞 𝄞 𝄞 𝄞

	1			6	7			
5				9			2	8
9	3	4						
	7		6					9
3				1				2
1					9		3	
						2	6	1
6	8			7				5
			5	2			7	

Difficulty rating: 🌿🌿🌿🌿🌿

158

	3		8	9			4	
4			3	5			1	
				4	7	9		
				6		8		
8		4	9	1	2	7		6
		9		8				
		5	6	7				
	1			2	4			9
	4			3	8		7	

Difficulty rating: 🍃🍃🍃🍃🍃

			2	9	8			1
9				5		8		
6		2		1				7
	5					4		
			1	6	7			
		7					8	
7				2		6		4
		1		3				8
4			6	7	9			

Difficulty rating: 🖋🖋🖋🖋🖋

160

2				4	6			1
	7		2	3			5	
	5	6		1				
5	2					4		
	4		6	7	2		9	
		9					7	8
				8		6	2	
	6			2	5		1	
7			1	6				4

Difficulty rating: 🍃🍃🍃🍃🍃

		4		2	8	9		
5				7				
		8		5	6			1
	3				1		5	
9				6				8
	5		2				1	
4			6	3		1		
				1				3
		7	5	4		8		

Difficulty rating: 🖋🖋🖋🖋🖋

		3		6		5	7	
			7	3				
	2		4	8			9	
		2		4			1	3
		8				9		
9	6			1		2		
	8			7	2		3	
				5	3			
	7	5		9		8		

Difficulty rating:

				4	2			5
	3			5				
6			7	3				2
	7			8			2	
		4	5		9	8		
	9			2			5	
2				1	4			8
				9			4	
5			2	7				

Difficulty rating:

5	2			8				
	7			3	6	5		1
			1	2			8	9
		2			4			
7				5				3
			6			8		
6	5			4	1			
9		3	8	6			5	
				9			6	4

Difficulty rating: 🍃🍃🍃🍃🍃

165

					6		7	
				1		6	9	
8			4					2
	9	2		4			6	
	3	7		2		1	4	
	8			6		2	5	
9					3			7
	2	8		5				
	6		1					

Difficulty rating: 🍃🍃🍃🍃🍃

				5			2	
5		3	4			8		
				9		1	5	
						9		2
		5	1	7	8	4		
4		7						
	5	8		3				
		2			4	7		3
	7			8				

Difficulty rating: 🌿🌿🌿🌿🌿

1				7			6	8
	9				6	1		
			8	1				5
2				8	9			
	4			6			3	
			3	4				2
9				5	8			
		1	6				8	
4	6			2				7

Difficulty rating: 🖊🖊🖊🖊🖊

168

			7	8	6	4		
				2			6	
				3	9			7
	2				8	9		
4	1	3		7		6	8	5
		9	3				2	
6			4	1				
	5			9				
		8	2	6	3			

Difficulty rating: 🍃🍃🍃🍃🍃

8					5		9	
	5			7	1	3		
		9	3		8		5	
		7		9		1		6
2								9
6		1		3		4		
	6		2		3	9		
	3	1	4				6	
	2		7					3

Difficulty rating: 🍃🍃🍃🍃🍃

					6		5	9
				9	4		2	
4	5			2	8	3		
							7	6
		7				2		
5	1							
		1	2	4			8	5
	8		1	5				
7	9		6					

Difficulty rating: 🖋🖋🖋🖋🖋

				3	6	2	1	
					1	7		
1			4			5		
3	6					1	7	
				5				
	8	5					4	2
		2			3			9
		1	6					
	3	6	8	9				

Difficulty rating: 🍃🍃🍃🍃🍃

3	9				2	7		
				5			2	
	6				7			4
			7	1				5
		8		2		3		
6				9	3			
1		6					9	
	2			4				
		5	2				4	7

Difficulty rating:

		6	5	9	3			
9	5		7	1				
	7			6				3
				5			2	4
	3	2		7		1	5	
5	9			8				
8				4			3	
				2	5		8	7
			8	3	7	2		

Difficulty rating: 🖋🖋🖋🖋🖋

174

	6				1			
		5	8	3		4		6
				4	5		8	
9		6		7				8
				2				
4				6		3		9
	4		9	1				
7		8		5	2	9		
			7				2	

Difficulty rating: 🍃🍃🍃🍃🍃

	1				4		8	
8		7		1	2			
2				5		6		
		1		6			4	8
				3				
7	6			4		2		
		3		2				4
			4	8		9		5
	8		9				6	

Difficulty rating: 🌿🌿🌿🌿🌿

2				9				
		3		8	6	9	4	
		4	3	2			7	8
	6	2		7		8	5	
				1				
	7	8		3		2	9	
8	4			6	3	7		
	3	7	8	4		6		
				5				3

Difficulty rating: 🖊🖊🖊🖊🖊

4				2		1		
	5		7				2	
	3		4	8	9			
		4		5				2
	1	7		9		4	5	
5				4		7		
			3	6	2		8	
	2				8		4	
		1		7				3

Difficulty rating: 🍃🍃🍃🍃🍃

6	4			9	3		1	
				5				
					6		5	4
	9			3		5		7
		2		6		8		
8		6		7			4	
7	2		6					
				2				
	6		1	8			3	5

Difficulty rating: 🖋🖋🖋🖋🖋

			6	9				1
				2	1		9	4
			3	7		2		
3						1		2
2	1			3			4	8
6		4						9
		2		6	8			
9	4		1	5				
5				4	7			

Difficulty rating: 🍃🍃🍃🍃🍃

180

				7	2	9		4
4						3		
			4					2
2				6	1			7
			3		5			
1			7	4				8
3					7			
		5						9
7		6	9	5				

Difficulty rating: 🌿🌿🌿🌿🌿

			5	6		8	4	
	6			4				
		8		9	7			1
			4					5
1		4		8		6		7
8					6			
6			8	7		2		
				3			9	
	7	9		5	4			

Difficulty rating: 🖋🖋🖋🖋🖋

	4		9	3				
					4			5
		3		8		1		2
3				6		8		
		9		7		4		
		7		1				9
8		5		4		2		
9			7					
				9	3		1	

Difficulty rating: 🌿🌿🌿🌿🌿

8		5	2				3	
				9	3			
7				1				
4		3		6				
	7	2		5		8	1	
				8		2		3
				2				7
			5	3				
	5				6	9		2

Difficulty rating: 🖊🖊🖊🖊🖊

184

3			8	9			7		
				6	7			1	
				4			5		
		3						4	
		4	1	5	9	3			
	5					8			
		6		3					
	9		5	7					
		7		1	8		9		

Difficulty rating: 🍃🍃🍃🍃🍃

				8	3			
	6		2	5				8
		1		9			3	2
	3							5
		9		1		7		
5							9	
8	1			6		4		
6				7	5		2	
			8	2				

Difficulty rating: 🖋 🖋 🖋 🖋 🖋

186

9			2	8	1	4		
	6			7				
4					9			7
	8		9			6		
5				4				9
		4			6		8	
1			3					5
				5			9	
		8	4	9	7			1

Difficulty rating: 🖊 🖊 🖊 🖊 🖊

		9		1	7			
3						8		
	8	4		9				1
8			5	7			6	
		6		8		2		
	7			2	1			4
2				4		6	3	
		8						2
			7	6		5		

Difficulty rating: 🖋🖋🖋🖋🖋

6				9	8	2		7
	8		3	5			4	
				2		1	8	6
				7				
4	5	2		8				
	9			4	2		6	
3		7	6	1				5

Difficulty rating: ✏✏✏✏✏

					5			4
3				7				
		9	2	1		5	6	
	5			2		8	1	
		3		8		7		
	1	7		9			4	
	7	6		5	2	9		
				6				5
5			3					

Difficulty rating: 🖋🖋🖋🖋🖋

190

					6			
9	8			3			2	
	3	1		2		8		
		9		4	2			7
				8				
4			7	5		1		
		3		9		5	7	
	4			6			8	9
			3					

Difficulty rating: ∂∂∂∂∂

	7	8			4			
9			7	1	8		2	
		2				1		
	1				9			6
4				8				1
3			1				9	
		4				5		
	5		8	3	7			4
			4			8	1	

Difficulty rating: 🖋🖋🖋🖋🖋

192

				3		7		
			7	2		5		6
				5	6		8	4
3				6		1	7	
	5						2	
	2	7		1				8
7	8		4	9				
1		6		7	5			
		9		8				

Difficulty rating: 🖋 🖋 🖋 🖋 🖋

9						3		
	5			3	1		7	
			8		4	9		
6		8		5			4	
				4				
	4			9		1		6
		2	4		6			
	8		3	7			9	
		7						5

Difficulty rating: 🍃🍃🍃🍃🍃

4				3	7	5		2
				9				
		3		2	8			
	8	9						7
6	3	2		7		8	5	4
7						9	3	
			8	1		6		
				5				
8		7	9	4				5

Difficulty rating: 🖋🖋🖋🖋🖋

			8	5		2	3	
	1	8		6	2			
								8
		5	9				1	
	9			1			6	
	2				3	9		
7								
			5	3		6	7	
	4	1		2	7			

Difficulty rating: 🖊🖊🖊🖊🖊

6			1		7		9	
3					8	6	2	
				2			3	
					3	2		4
4				6				9
2		8	7					
	4			5				
	6	3	8					1
	5		3		9			2

Difficulty rating: 🖊🖊🖊🖊🖊

			3				9	
				1	9		6	
				5		3		8
		5			3	8		
4	9			7			1	5
		6	1			9		
9		2		6				
	5		4	8				
	6				7			

Difficulty rating: 🖋🖋🖋🖋🖋

3				4	9	2		1
	8						7	
4			8	3				
		2				1		4
				5				
9		8				5		
				8	5			9
	7						3	
8		3	2	1				5

Difficulty rating: 🖊🖊🖊🖊🖊

4				1	2			6
				8		1		
			6	7		3		5
							8	
	3	6		5		2	1	
	1							
1		5		4	7			
		4		2				
6			1	3				7

Difficulty rating: 🖋🖋🖋🖋🖋

200

		2	9	8	7			
	4			5		3		1
5								
1			6				7	
		4		2		1		
	7				8			6
								8
7		9		1			3	
			8	6	2	7		

Difficulty rating: 🍃🍃🍃🍃🍃

SOLUTIONS

1

5	1	8	7	2	4	6	9	3
2	3	6	5	8	9	4	7	1
9	7	4	6	3	1	8	2	5
8	6	7	9	5	2	3	1	4
3	2	9	4	1	6	5	8	7
1	4	5	8	7	3	2	6	9
6	5	1	2	4	7	9	3	8
4	9	3	1	6	8	7	5	2
7	8	2	3	9	5	1	4	6

2

7	4	3	5	9	2	8	6	1
9	8	1	6	7	4	2	5	3
6	2	5	3	8	1	9	4	7
1	7	2	9	5	3	6	8	4
3	6	4	8	2	7	1	9	5
8	5	9	1	4	6	3	7	2
2	9	7	4	1	8	5	3	6
4	3	8	2	6	5	7	1	9
5	1	6	7	3	9	4	2	8

3

7	9	8	1	5	3	4	6	2
6	2	5	4	9	7	8	3	1
3	1	4	8	2	6	7	9	5
5	8	9	7	4	2	3	1	6
2	7	3	5	6	1	9	8	4
1	4	6	3	8	9	5	2	7
9	5	7	2	1	8	6	4	3
8	3	1	6	7	4	2	5	9
4	6	2	9	3	5	1	7	8

4

2	3	8	6	7	4	5	1	9
9	6	4	2	1	5	3	7	8
1	5	7	3	8	9	2	4	6
3	2	1	9	5	7	8	6	4
6	4	9	8	3	2	7	5	1
8	7	5	4	6	1	9	2	3
5	1	3	7	9	6	4	8	2
7	8	2	1	4	3	6	9	5
4	9	6	5	2	8	1	3	7

5

3	6	1	7	4	5	8	2	9
9	7	8	1	2	6	5	3	4
2	4	5	3	9	8	6	7	1
6	1	9	4	7	2	3	8	5
4	8	2	9	5	3	7	1	6
7	5	3	6	8	1	9	4	2
5	2	4	8	3	9	1	6	7
8	9	6	2	1	7	4	5	3
1	3	7	5	6	4	2	9	8

6

5	6	7	3	8	9	2	4	1
3	1	9	4	6	2	8	7	5
2	8	4	5	1	7	9	6	3
1	3	2	9	4	8	6	5	7
4	5	6	2	7	3	1	9	8
7	9	8	6	5	1	3	2	4
8	7	5	1	2	6	4	3	9
6	4	3	8	9	5	7	1	2
9	2	1	7	3	4	5	8	6

7

6	4	8	1	3	2	9	5	7
1	9	5	8	4	7	6	3	2
2	7	3	6	5	9	8	1	4
5	3	1	7	2	8	4	9	6
7	2	9	4	1	6	5	8	3
4	8	6	3	9	5	2	7	1
3	6	4	5	8	1	7	2	9
9	5	7	2	6	3	1	4	8
8	1	2	9	7	4	3	6	5

8

1	5	9	6	3	2	4	8	7
8	2	7	1	5	4	3	6	9
3	6	4	8	9	7	5	1	2
7	3	8	4	6	1	2	9	5
9	1	2	7	8	5	6	3	4
6	4	5	3	2	9	8	7	1
2	8	1	5	7	3	9	4	6
4	9	3	2	1	6	7	5	8
5	7	6	9	4	8	1	2	3

9

5	4	2	8	7	3	1	9	6
8	9	3	6	5	1	2	7	4
6	7	1	4	9	2	8	3	5
4	1	6	3	8	5	7	2	9
3	8	9	7	2	4	5	6	1
7	2	5	9	1	6	3	4	8
1	5	7	2	6	9	4	8	3
2	6	4	5	3	8	9	1	7
9	3	8	1	4	7	6	5	2

10

2	6	5	7	4	9	1	3	8
1	7	9	6	3	8	4	2	5
8	3	4	5	2	1	7	6	9
9	8	3	1	5	2	6	7	4
5	4	6	9	7	3	8	1	2
7	1	2	4	8	6	5	9	3
3	5	1	8	9	7	2	4	6
4	2	7	3	6	5	9	8	1
6	9	8	2	1	4	3	5	7

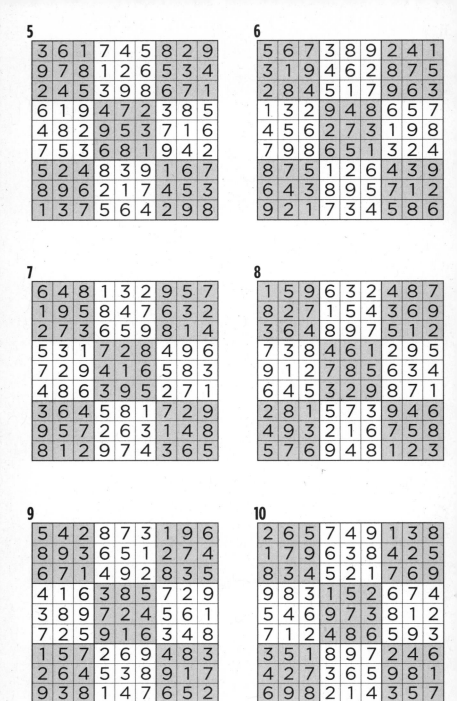

11

7	6	3	8	1	4	9	5	2
8	9	4	3	2	5	6	1	7
5	1	2	6	9	7	8	4	3
6	4	8	7	5	2	3	9	1
2	3	9	1	6	8	5	7	4
1	5	7	4	3	9	2	8	6
9	8	1	2	7	3	4	6	5
3	7	5	9	4	6	1	2	8
4	2	6	5	8	1	7	3	9

12

2	3	7	6	5	8	4	1	9
9	4	1	3	2	7	6	8	5
8	5	6	9	4	1	7	3	2
7	9	8	5	3	6	1	2	4
1	2	5	7	8	4	9	6	3
4	6	3	2	1	9	5	7	8
3	7	2	4	6	5	8	9	1
5	8	9	1	7	3	2	4	6
6	1	4	8	9	2	3	5	7

13

5	6	4	8	3	7	2	9	1
9	2	7	1	4	5	8	3	6
8	1	3	2	6	9	5	4	7
6	4	1	5	7	8	3	2	9
2	9	5	6	1	3	7	8	4
7	3	8	4	9	2	1	6	5
4	5	6	3	8	1	9	7	2
3	7	2	9	5	6	4	1	8
1	8	9	7	2	4	6	5	3

14

1	9	7	6	4	8	5	2	3
5	4	3	9	7	2	8	1	6
8	2	6	3	1	5	9	4	7
2	5	1	8	9	7	3	6	4
7	3	9	1	6	4	2	5	8
6	8	4	5	2	3	7	9	1
3	6	2	7	5	1	4	8	9
9	7	5	4	8	6	1	3	2
4	1	8	2	3	9	6	7	5

15

6	1	3	8	5	9	2	4	7
9	7	4	2	6	3	8	1	5
2	8	5	1	4	7	3	9	6
4	9	7	3	2	1	6	5	8
8	3	6	9	7	5	1	2	4
5	2	1	4	8	6	9	7	3
7	6	9	5	3	2	4	8	1
3	4	2	7	1	8	5	6	9
1	5	8	6	9	4	7	3	2

16

4	8	5	1	2	7	3	6	9
2	6	7	4	3	9	5	1	8
1	3	9	8	6	5	7	2	4
3	1	2	6	4	8	9	5	7
5	7	6	3	9	2	4	8	1
9	4	8	5	7	1	6	3	2
7	9	1	2	5	3	8	4	6
6	2	3	7	8	4	1	9	5
8	5	4	9	1	6	2	7	3

17

1	2	3	9	5	4	8	6	7
6	7	8	3	1	2	4	5	9
9	5	4	7	6	8	2	1	3
4	9	6	2	7	5	1	3	8
8	3	2	1	4	6	7	9	5
5	1	7	8	3	9	6	2	4
7	4	9	5	2	1	3	8	6
2	6	5	4	8	3	9	7	1
3	8	1	6	9	7	5	4	2

18

9	3	1	4	5	6	2	7	8
5	4	8	3	7	2	1	9	6
2	7	6	9	1	8	4	5	3
3	6	4	8	9	1	7	2	5
7	9	2	6	3	5	8	4	1
8	1	5	2	4	7	6	3	9
6	8	3	7	2	9	5	1	4
1	2	9	5	8	4	3	6	7
4	5	7	1	6	3	9	8	2

19

9	5	6	4	7	8	1	2	3
1	8	7	6	3	2	5	4	9
3	2	4	5	1	9	7	6	8
8	3	2	9	5	4	6	7	1
6	7	1	2	8	3	4	9	5
5	4	9	7	6	1	3	8	2
7	9	3	8	4	5	2	1	6
4	1	8	3	2	6	9	5	7
2	6	5	1	9	7	8	3	4

20

2	6	9	8	5	4	3	1	7
1	4	5	3	9	7	8	6	2
3	8	7	2	6	1	9	5	4
6	2	1	9	7	3	5	4	8
5	7	3	4	8	2	6	9	1
8	9	4	5	1	6	7	2	3
9	5	2	1	3	8	4	7	6
7	1	8	6	4	9	2	3	5
4	3	6	7	2	5	1	8	9

21

2	1	6	9	5	3	4	8	7
4	3	5	8	7	6	1	2	9
8	9	7	4	2	1	5	3	6
9	8	1	5	6	7	2	4	3
6	2	4	3	1	8	9	7	5
7	5	3	2	9	4	8	6	1
3	6	9	1	4	2	7	5	8
1	7	2	6	8	5	3	9	4
5	4	8	7	3	9	6	1	2

22

1	4	6	3	5	7	9	8	2
7	5	2	6	9	8	1	3	4
8	9	3	2	1	4	7	6	5
6	7	5	9	8	2	3	4	1
4	3	9	1	7	6	5	2	8
2	1	8	4	3	5	6	7	9
5	6	7	8	4	9	2	1	3
3	2	4	5	6	1	8	9	7
9	8	1	7	2	3	4	5	6

23

7	5	1	9	3	4	2	6	8
6	9	4	8	2	7	5	1	3
2	3	8	5	1	6	9	7	4
9	7	5	1	4	2	8	3	6
3	4	2	7	6	8	1	5	9
8	1	6	3	9	5	7	4	2
4	2	7	6	8	1	3	9	5
1	6	9	2	5	3	4	8	7
5	8	3	4	7	9	6	2	1

24

5	7	3	4	8	9	2	6	1
1	6	4	2	3	5	8	7	9
8	2	9	6	1	7	3	4	5
9	4	8	3	5	6	7	1	2
7	1	2	8	9	4	6	5	3
3	5	6	1	7	2	4	9	8
6	8	5	7	2	1	9	3	4
4	3	1	9	6	8	5	2	7
2	9	7	5	4	3	1	8	6

25

6	2	4	9	7	5	8	1	3
5	7	3	6	1	8	2	4	9
1	8	9	4	2	3	5	7	6
9	4	7	8	3	6	1	2	5
2	3	1	5	9	7	4	6	8
8	5	6	2	4	1	3	9	7
3	9	5	1	6	4	7	8	2
4	6	8	7	5	2	9	3	1
7	1	2	3	8	9	6	5	4

26

8	5	9	1	2	7	3	6	4
1	7	2	6	3	4	9	8	5
6	3	4	9	8	5	7	2	1
5	4	1	2	7	8	6	3	9
7	2	3	4	6	9	1	5	8
9	6	8	3	5	1	4	7	2
4	8	6	7	9	2	5	1	3
2	1	7	5	4	3	8	9	6
3	9	5	8	1	6	2	4	7

27

5	2	8	1	4	7	6	9	3
7	4	9	2	3	6	8	1	5
6	3	1	9	5	8	2	4	7
3	6	7	5	9	1	4	2	8
4	9	5	7	8	2	3	6	1
8	1	2	4	6	3	7	5	9
1	5	6	8	7	4	9	3	2
9	8	3	6	2	5	1	7	4
2	7	4	3	1	9	5	8	6

28

4	9	2	6	3	5	7	1	8
8	3	5	4	1	7	9	2	6
6	1	7	9	8	2	4	3	5
2	4	1	8	7	3	5	6	9
9	7	3	1	5	6	2	8	4
5	8	6	2	9	4	3	7	1
7	5	8	3	6	9	1	4	2
1	2	9	7	4	8	6	5	3
3	6	4	5	2	1	8	9	7

29

7	6	3	2	9	5	4	1	8
5	2	9	4	1	8	3	6	7
1	8	4	6	7	3	2	9	5
3	1	8	7	6	9	5	4	2
4	9	6	8	5	2	7	3	1
2	7	5	1	3	4	6	8	9
8	4	1	3	2	7	9	5	6
9	3	7	5	8	6	1	2	4
6	5	2	9	4	1	8	7	3

30

9	6	8	3	4	1	5	2	7
7	1	2	5	6	8	9	3	4
5	4	3	7	9	2	8	1	6
4	9	6	8	2	3	7	5	1
3	8	1	9	7	5	6	4	2
2	7	5	4	1	6	3	9	8
6	3	9	2	8	4	1	7	5
1	2	7	6	5	9	4	8	3
8	5	4	1	3	7	2	6	9

31

7	8	5	6	4	2	3	1	9
2	4	9	7	1	3	8	5	6
6	1	3	8	5	9	2	7	4
3	7	1	9	8	6	5	4	2
8	5	4	2	7	1	9	6	3
9	6	2	5	3	4	7	8	1
4	3	8	1	9	7	6	2	5
5	9	6	4	2	8	1	3	7
1	2	7	3	6	5	4	9	8

32

8	3	4	2	1	5	9	6	7
1	9	2	8	7	6	4	3	5
7	6	5	3	9	4	1	8	2
2	8	6	4	5	1	7	9	3
5	1	3	7	2	9	8	4	6
9	4	7	6	8	3	5	2	1
4	5	1	9	6	2	3	7	8
3	2	8	5	4	7	6	1	9
6	7	9	1	3	8	2	5	4

33

5	4	3	7	6	1	2	9	8
1	6	7	2	9	8	5	3	4
2	8	9	3	5	4	1	7	6
6	9	5	8	7	2	4	1	3
4	3	8	9	1	6	7	2	5
7	2	1	5	4	3	8	6	9
8	1	4	6	3	7	9	5	2
3	5	2	1	8	9	6	4	7
9	7	6	4	2	5	3	8	1

34

6	3	4	5	1	8	9	2	7
8	7	5	4	9	2	6	3	1
9	2	1	6	3	7	4	5	8
2	8	7	3	6	5	1	9	4
3	1	9	7	2	4	5	8	6
5	4	6	1	8	9	3	7	2
4	5	8	9	7	6	2	1	3
7	6	3	2	5	1	8	4	9
1	9	2	8	4	3	7	6	5

35

6	5	7	4	8	1	2	3	9
4	2	1	5	9	3	8	7	6
3	9	8	2	7	6	5	4	1
7	4	5	8	3	9	1	6	2
2	6	9	1	5	7	3	8	4
1	8	3	6	4	2	7	9	5
5	7	4	9	1	8	6	2	3
9	3	2	7	6	5	4	1	8
8	1	6	3	2	4	9	5	7

36

4	3	5	8	2	1	6	9	7
2	6	8	9	4	7	1	5	3
9	7	1	6	3	5	8	2	4
6	9	4	1	5	2	3	7	8
5	8	2	7	6	3	9	4	1
3	1	7	4	9	8	5	6	2
8	2	3	5	7	9	4	1	6
1	4	9	2	8	6	7	3	5
7	5	6	3	1	4	2	8	9

37

9	4	7	3	8	2	5	1	6
2	3	8	6	5	1	7	4	9
5	6	1	7	9	4	3	8	2
7	1	9	2	4	8	6	3	5
6	8	3	5	1	7	2	9	4
4	5	2	9	3	6	8	7	1
1	2	4	8	6	3	9	5	7
3	7	5	1	2	9	4	6	8
8	9	6	4	7	5	1	2	3

38

2	5	7	9	8	1	6	4	3
9	4	8	7	3	6	1	5	2
3	6	1	2	4	5	7	9	8
8	2	9	6	7	3	5	1	4
1	7	4	8	5	2	3	6	9
5	3	6	4	1	9	2	8	7
4	8	2	5	6	7	9	3	1
7	1	5	3	9	8	4	2	6
6	9	3	1	2	4	8	7	5

39

8	5	9	1	3	7	2	4	6
2	3	1	6	4	5	9	8	7
4	7	6	9	8	2	1	3	5
6	2	7	5	1	4	8	9	3
9	1	3	8	2	6	7	5	4
5	8	4	7	9	3	6	1	2
3	6	8	2	5	1	4	7	9
1	4	2	3	7	9	5	6	8
7	9	5	4	6	8	3	2	1

40

9	4	5	1	2	3	6	7	8
8	6	1	9	4	7	2	3	5
3	7	2	6	8	5	1	4	9
7	3	4	5	1	9	8	2	6
6	1	8	3	7	2	9	5	4
2	5	9	4	6	8	7	1	3
1	9	7	8	3	4	5	6	2
5	2	3	7	9	6	4	8	1
4	8	6	2	5	1	3	9	7

41

1	8	4	2	3	5	7	9	6
3	5	2	9	7	6	1	8	4
6	7	9	4	1	8	5	2	3
5	6	3	7	4	9	8	1	2
9	2	7	6	8	1	3	4	5
8	4	1	5	2	3	6	7	9
4	3	8	1	5	2	9	6	7
7	1	6	3	9	4	2	5	8
2	9	5	8	6	7	4	3	1

42

6	5	3	7	2	4	8	1	9
2	7	8	5	1	9	3	4	6
1	9	4	3	6	8	5	7	2
3	2	5	9	4	7	6	8	1
7	6	1	8	5	2	4	9	3
4	8	9	6	3	1	7	2	5
9	3	7	2	8	6	1	5	4
5	4	2	1	7	3	9	6	8
8	1	6	4	9	5	2	3	7

43

1	7	3	2	5	6	8	4	9
8	2	9	3	1	4	7	5	6
6	4	5	9	8	7	1	3	2
3	6	1	5	4	2	9	7	8
2	8	4	1	7	9	3	6	5
5	9	7	6	3	8	4	2	1
7	3	6	8	2	1	5	9	4
9	5	8	4	6	3	2	1	7
4	1	2	7	9	5	6	8	3

44

2	8	9	7	3	6	1	5	4
1	5	4	9	8	2	6	3	7
3	6	7	5	4	1	8	9	2
6	9	1	2	7	5	3	4	8
5	3	2	4	1	8	9	7	6
4	7	8	3	6	9	2	1	5
9	4	6	8	5	3	7	2	1
8	2	5	1	9	7	4	6	3
7	1	3	6	2	4	5	8	9

45

7	1	3	5	4	6	2	9	8
8	2	4	3	9	7	5	1	6
9	5	6	2	8	1	3	7	4
3	6	9	8	1	2	4	5	7
4	7	2	9	3	5	6	8	1
5	8	1	6	7	4	9	2	3
2	3	5	1	6	8	7	4	9
1	9	7	4	5	3	8	6	2
6	4	8	7	2	9	1	3	5

46

6	7	2	5	3	8	1	9	4
5	3	4	7	9	1	2	8	6
8	1	9	4	2	6	3	7	5
7	5	1	2	8	4	6	3	9
9	4	6	3	5	7	8	1	2
2	8	3	1	6	9	4	5	7
1	9	8	6	4	5	7	2	3
3	6	7	9	1	2	5	4	8
4	2	5	8	7	3	9	6	1

47

9	6	5	3	1	2	7	8	4
1	2	4	8	9	7	6	3	5
3	8	7	5	4	6	1	9	2
8	1	2	9	7	4	5	6	3
6	5	9	1	3	8	4	2	7
7	4	3	2	6	5	8	1	9
2	9	8	7	5	1	3	4	6
5	3	6	4	8	9	2	7	1
4	7	1	6	2	3	9	5	8

48

5	6	3	1	7	4	8	2	9
4	1	9	2	5	8	3	6	7
7	2	8	6	3	9	5	4	1
2	5	6	9	8	3	1	7	4
1	3	7	4	2	5	6	9	8
8	9	4	7	6	1	2	5	3
6	4	2	3	1	7	9	8	5
9	8	1	5	4	2	7	3	6
3	7	5	8	9	6	4	1	2

49

9	6	1	2	3	7	4	5	8
8	5	4	1	6	9	3	2	7
7	3	2	4	5	8	6	1	9
1	2	7	8	4	6	5	9	3
3	8	9	7	2	5	1	4	6
5	4	6	9	1	3	7	8	2
2	9	3	5	7	1	8	6	4
6	1	8	3	9	4	2	7	5
4	7	5	6	8	2	9	3	1

50

1	4	9	2	5	8	7	3	6
8	3	7	9	6	4	5	1	2
5	6	2	3	7	1	8	4	9
9	1	3	4	8	5	6	2	7
6	7	8	1	2	3	4	9	5
4	2	5	6	9	7	3	8	1
2	8	6	7	4	9	1	5	3
3	9	4	5	1	6	2	7	8
7	5	1	8	3	2	9	6	4

51

8	5	4	3	2	6	7	1	9
3	2	6	9	1	7	8	4	5
1	7	9	4	5	8	2	3	6
7	6	3	1	4	5	9	8	2
4	9	1	6	8	2	3	5	7
2	8	5	7	9	3	4	6	1
9	3	2	5	6	4	1	7	8
6	4	8	2	7	1	5	9	3
5	1	7	8	3	9	6	2	4

52

7	9	8	4	1	6	5	2	3
5	6	4	7	3	2	1	9	8
1	3	2	9	5	8	4	7	6
8	2	7	1	6	4	9	3	5
9	4	1	5	7	3	6	8	2
3	5	6	8	2	9	7	1	4
2	7	3	6	4	1	8	5	9
4	1	9	3	8	5	2	6	7
6	8	5	2	9	7	3	4	1

53

1	2	7	8	3	5	4	9	6
5	6	3	4	2	9	7	8	1
9	4	8	6	7	1	5	2	3
6	8	9	3	4	2	1	7	5
3	5	1	9	8	7	6	4	2
4	7	2	1	5	6	8	3	9
8	9	6	7	1	3	2	5	4
2	3	4	5	6	8	9	1	7
7	1	5	2	9	4	3	6	8

54

1	8	7	6	5	2	3	9	4
2	9	3	4	7	8	6	5	1
4	5	6	3	1	9	7	2	8
9	1	8	2	6	5	4	7	3
7	2	4	1	8	3	5	6	9
3	6	5	7	9	4	1	8	2
5	3	9	8	4	6	2	1	7
6	7	2	9	3	1	8	4	5
8	4	1	5	2	7	9	3	6

55

8	1	3	5	4	9	2	7	6
6	5	7	2	8	3	9	4	1
2	9	4	1	7	6	5	8	3
9	8	1	3	2	4	6	5	7
5	7	2	9	6	1	4	3	8
3	4	6	8	5	7	1	2	9
1	3	8	4	9	5	7	6	2
4	6	9	7	3	2	8	1	5
7	2	5	6	1	8	3	9	4

56

4	9	8	2	7	3	5	1	6
5	6	3	9	8	1	4	2	7
1	2	7	4	5	6	9	8	3
2	8	6	3	1	4	7	5	9
9	4	5	6	2	7	8	3	1
3	7	1	8	9	5	6	4	2
6	5	2	7	3	8	1	9	4
7	1	9	5	4	2	3	6	8
8	3	4	1	6	9	2	7	5

57

5	6	1	9	2	7	4	3	8
2	9	7	8	3	4	6	1	5
8	4	3	6	1	5	7	9	2
4	8	6	7	9	2	1	5	3
7	5	2	3	8	1	9	4	6
3	1	9	5	4	6	2	8	7
9	2	5	4	6	3	8	7	1
1	3	8	2	7	9	5	6	4
6	7	4	1	5	8	3	2	9

58

1	9	8	5	7	4	3	6	2
3	6	7	9	8	2	1	4	5
4	2	5	6	3	1	7	8	9
7	1	2	3	5	8	6	9	4
9	8	3	4	1	6	5	2	7
5	4	6	2	9	7	8	1	3
8	3	1	7	4	9	2	5	6
6	5	4	1	2	3	9	7	8
2	7	9	8	6	5	4	3	1

59

2	9	7	3	4	5	6	1	8
4	6	1	7	2	8	5	9	3
8	3	5	1	6	9	4	7	2
6	2	4	5	8	7	9	3	1
1	8	3	4	9	2	7	6	5
5	7	9	6	3	1	2	8	4
7	5	2	9	1	3	8	4	6
9	1	6	8	5	4	3	2	7
3	4	8	2	7	6	1	5	9

60

4	7	3	2	5	8	9	1	6
9	1	6	7	3	4	2	8	5
2	8	5	6	1	9	4	7	3
1	5	2	3	4	6	7	9	8
7	4	9	5	8	1	6	3	2
6	3	8	9	7	2	1	5	4
5	9	4	1	6	3	8	2	7
3	6	1	8	2	7	5	4	9
8	2	7	4	9	5	3	6	1

61

9	1	7	6	2	4	5	3	8
3	5	2	7	1	8	4	6	9
8	4	6	9	3	5	2	7	1
4	8	1	5	6	3	9	2	7
5	6	3	2	9	7	1	8	4
2	7	9	8	4	1	6	5	3
6	2	4	3	8	9	7	1	5
1	3	5	4	7	2	8	9	6
7	9	8	1	5	6	3	4	2

62

8	1	2	3	5	6	7	9	4
6	5	9	7	8	4	1	2	3
3	7	4	9	1	2	5	6	8
1	2	8	5	4	3	6	7	9
5	4	7	8	6	9	3	1	2
9	3	6	1	2	7	8	4	5
4	6	5	2	3	1	9	8	7
2	9	3	6	7	8	4	5	1
7	8	1	4	9	5	2	3	6

63

8	1	7	9	2	3	5	4	6
6	9	4	5	8	1	7	3	2
3	5	2	7	6	4	1	9	8
9	8	6	2	7	5	3	1	4
1	2	5	4	3	8	9	6	7
7	4	3	6	1	9	8	2	5
2	6	8	1	9	7	4	5	3
4	3	1	8	5	2	6	7	9
5	7	9	3	4	6	2	8	1

64

2	5	9	7	8	1	4	3	6
6	7	8	4	5	3	1	2	9
4	3	1	9	6	2	5	8	7
3	8	5	1	4	7	6	9	2
9	1	2	6	3	5	8	7	4
7	4	6	2	9	8	3	1	5
1	9	4	3	7	6	2	5	8
5	6	3	8	2	9	7	4	1
8	2	7	5	1	4	9	6	3

65

1	8	5	7	4	9	2	3	6
6	4	7	3	1	2	9	8	5
9	3	2	5	8	6	1	4	7
8	2	1	9	7	3	5	6	4
5	9	6	8	2	4	3	7	1
3	7	4	1	6	5	8	2	9
2	6	9	4	3	1	7	5	8
7	1	3	6	5	8	4	9	2
4	5	8	2	9	7	6	1	3

66

1	7	5	6	8	2	9	3	4
3	2	9	5	1	4	6	7	8
8	4	6	7	3	9	5	2	1
4	6	1	2	9	3	8	5	7
9	8	3	4	5	7	1	6	2
2	5	7	8	6	1	3	4	9
6	3	2	9	7	8	4	1	5
7	1	8	3	4	5	2	9	6
5	9	4	1	2	6	7	8	3

67

9	2	8	1	3	5	6	7	4
5	7	3	6	4	8	1	2	9
4	1	6	7	9	2	5	8	3
8	4	7	9	1	6	3	5	2
3	9	1	5	2	4	7	6	8
2	6	5	3	8	7	4	9	1
6	3	9	2	5	1	8	4	7
1	5	4	8	7	9	2	3	6
7	8	2	4	6	3	9	1	5

68

1	5	9	7	2	6	4	8	3
7	8	4	1	9	3	2	5	6
2	6	3	4	8	5	9	1	7
6	7	5	9	1	4	8	3	2
9	3	1	8	6	2	5	7	4
8	4	2	5	3	7	6	9	1
3	1	6	2	5	8	7	4	9
4	2	8	3	7	9	1	6	5
5	9	7	6	4	1	3	2	8

69

3	7	9	1	2	4	8	6	5
5	8	1	6	3	7	2	9	4
4	6	2	5	9	8	1	3	7
1	2	8	3	7	6	4	5	9
9	3	4	2	5	1	6	7	8
6	5	7	4	8	9	3	1	2
2	1	3	7	4	5	9	8	6
7	9	6	8	1	2	5	4	3
8	4	5	9	6	3	7	2	1

70

9	3	6	4	8	2	5	7	1
7	8	2	6	1	5	9	4	3
5	4	1	7	9	3	6	8	2
3	9	4	2	5	1	8	6	7
6	5	7	8	3	4	1	2	9
1	2	8	9	6	7	4	3	5
2	6	5	1	7	8	3	9	4
4	1	9	3	2	6	7	5	8
8	7	3	5	4	9	2	1	6

71

8	5	3	4	1	9	2	7	6
7	1	4	2	3	6	5	8	9
2	9	6	7	8	5	1	4	3
5	7	8	1	4	3	9	6	2
1	4	9	5	6	2	8	3	7
6	3	2	9	7	8	4	5	1
9	8	7	6	2	4	3	1	5
4	6	5	3	9	1	7	2	8
3	2	1	8	5	7	6	9	4

72

5	2	4	8	9	6	3	1	7
9	3	1	4	7	2	6	5	8
6	7	8	1	3	5	2	9	4
4	5	7	9	6	3	8	2	1
8	1	6	7	2	4	5	3	9
2	9	3	5	1	8	7	4	6
1	8	2	6	5	9	4	7	3
3	4	9	2	8	7	1	6	5
7	6	5	3	4	1	9	8	2

73

7	2	5	4	1	6	9	3	8
4	9	1	7	3	8	2	6	5
8	6	3	9	5	2	7	1	4
5	7	4	6	9	3	8	2	1
3	1	2	8	4	7	6	5	9
6	8	9	1	2	5	3	4	7
2	4	7	3	8	1	5	9	6
1	3	8	5	6	9	4	7	2
9	5	6	2	7	4	1	8	3

74

1	6	7	9	8	5	3	2	4
2	9	5	1	3	4	6	7	8
8	3	4	7	2	6	9	5	1
9	4	6	8	5	1	7	3	2
7	2	3	6	4	9	1	8	5
5	1	8	3	7	2	4	9	6
6	5	9	2	1	3	8	4	7
3	8	2	4	6	7	5	1	9
4	7	1	5	9	8	2	6	3

75

8	4	1	6	5	2	9	7	3
9	6	3	8	7	1	5	4	2
2	7	5	3	9	4	6	1	8
7	3	2	9	8	5	1	6	4
4	9	8	1	2	6	3	5	7
5	1	6	7	4	3	8	2	9
3	8	4	5	6	7	2	9	1
1	5	7	2	3	9	4	8	6
6	2	9	4	1	8	7	3	5

76

1	6	9	7	3	2	8	4	5
5	8	2	6	9	4	3	1	7
4	7	3	8	1	5	6	2	9
3	1	4	9	8	7	2	5	6
6	5	7	1	2	3	4	9	8
2	9	8	4	5	6	7	3	1
8	3	6	5	4	9	1	7	2
7	2	5	3	6	1	9	8	4
9	4	1	2	7	8	5	6	3

77

9	2	6	1	7	8	3	5	4
7	5	4	2	3	9	1	6	8
8	1	3	6	5	4	7	2	9
2	6	5	3	4	7	8	9	1
3	9	1	8	6	2	4	7	5
4	8	7	5	9	1	2	3	6
5	4	2	7	1	6	9	8	3
6	7	9	4	8	3	5	1	2
1	3	8	9	2	5	6	4	7

78

4	8	7	1	9	5	3	6	2
1	6	3	8	4	2	9	7	5
9	5	2	6	7	3	1	8	4
7	3	6	2	5	9	4	1	8
2	1	9	3	8	4	6	5	7
8	4	5	7	6	1	2	3	9
6	9	1	5	2	8	7	4	3
5	7	4	9	3	6	8	2	1
3	2	8	4	1	7	5	9	6

79

4	3	7	9	1	2	8	6	5
5	2	1	4	8	6	9	7	3
9	6	8	3	5	7	1	2	4
2	7	9	5	6	1	4	3	8
6	8	3	7	4	9	2	5	1
1	5	4	8	2	3	7	9	6
7	1	2	6	3	4	5	8	9
3	4	5	2	9	8	6	1	7
8	9	6	1	7	5	3	4	2

80

9	1	3	7	5	2	6	4	8
5	4	6	8	9	1	3	2	7
7	2	8	3	6	4	9	5	1
2	7	4	6	8	3	1	9	5
6	3	1	5	2	9	8	7	4
8	9	5	1	4	7	2	3	6
4	6	9	2	1	5	7	8	3
1	5	7	9	3	8	4	6	2
3	8	2	4	7	6	5	1	9

81

6	1	9	5	4	3	2	7	8
5	2	8	9	7	1	4	6	3
3	7	4	8	6	2	5	1	9
1	6	5	7	3	8	9	4	2
8	9	7	1	2	4	6	3	5
4	3	2	6	9	5	7	8	1
9	5	6	3	8	7	1	2	4
7	4	3	2	1	9	8	5	6
2	8	1	4	5	6	3	9	7

82

4	7	6	1	2	9	5	3	8
9	5	1	3	4	8	7	6	2
2	8	3	6	5	7	9	4	1
8	9	4	2	7	1	3	5	6
5	6	2	4	8	3	1	7	9
3	1	7	9	6	5	8	2	4
6	3	8	7	1	4	2	9	5
7	2	5	8	9	6	4	1	3
1	4	9	5	3	2	6	8	7

83

9	6	2	8	1	4	3	5	7
4	3	8	2	5	7	6	9	1
5	1	7	3	6	9	8	2	4
1	4	3	6	9	5	7	8	2
7	5	6	1	2	8	4	3	9
8	2	9	7	4	3	5	1	6
3	7	4	9	8	1	2	6	5
2	9	5	4	3	6	1	7	8
6	8	1	5	7	2	9	4	3

84

1	3	6	2	8	4	7	5	9
2	9	4	7	6	5	8	3	1
8	7	5	3	1	9	6	4	2
4	2	3	1	7	8	5	9	6
6	8	1	9	5	3	4	2	7
7	5	9	4	2	6	1	8	3
5	1	8	6	9	2	3	7	4
3	6	2	8	4	7	9	1	5
9	4	7	5	3	1	2	6	8

85

4	5	2	7	6	1	8	3	9
9	6	3	4	5	8	1	7	2
8	1	7	3	2	9	4	5	6
7	9	8	1	3	2	5	6	4
1	2	4	6	9	5	3	8	7
5	3	6	8	7	4	2	9	1
3	4	9	2	8	7	6	1	5
6	7	1	5	4	3	9	2	8
2	8	5	9	1	6	7	4	3

86

7	9	6	1	4	2	3	8	5
5	4	2	6	8	3	1	7	9
3	1	8	9	7	5	6	2	4
2	3	5	4	9	7	8	6	1
4	7	1	3	6	8	9	5	2
8	6	9	2	5	1	4	3	7
1	5	3	8	2	9	7	4	6
9	2	4	7	3	6	5	1	8
6	8	7	5	1	4	2	9	3

87

1	3	9	5	2	7	6	4	8
8	6	2	9	4	1	3	5	7
5	7	4	6	8	3	2	9	1
2	8	7	3	5	6	9	1	4
3	5	1	7	9	4	8	6	2
4	9	6	8	1	2	5	7	3
7	4	3	2	6	9	1	8	5
9	1	8	4	3	5	7	2	6
6	2	5	1	7	8	4	3	9

88

8	4	9	6	3	5	7	1	2
1	6	2	4	7	9	5	8	3
5	3	7	2	8	1	4	9	6
3	2	8	5	6	7	9	4	1
7	5	4	9	1	3	6	2	8
6	9	1	8	2	4	3	5	7
2	8	5	3	9	6	1	7	4
9	1	6	7	4	8	2	3	5
4	7	3	1	5	2	8	6	9

89

3	8	5	2	9	7	1	4	6
1	7	9	5	4	6	8	3	2
4	2	6	8	3	1	7	5	9
2	4	7	6	1	8	5	9	3
6	5	1	3	2	9	4	8	7
9	3	8	4	7	5	2	6	1
5	1	4	9	6	2	3	7	8
8	6	2	7	5	3	9	1	4
7	9	3	1	8	4	6	2	5

90

9	5	7	1	2	4	6	3	8
6	3	2	9	7	8	5	1	4
8	1	4	5	6	3	2	7	9
5	6	9	7	8	1	4	2	3
7	8	3	2	4	5	9	6	1
2	4	1	3	9	6	7	8	5
1	9	6	8	5	7	3	4	2
4	2	8	6	3	9	1	5	7
3	7	5	4	1	2	8	9	6

91

4	6	5	9	1	3	7	2	8
9	7	1	2	8	5	4	6	3
8	3	2	6	4	7	5	9	1
6	8	7	1	3	2	9	4	5
2	9	3	8	5	4	1	7	6
1	5	4	7	9	6	3	8	2
3	2	8	5	7	9	6	1	4
5	1	9	4	6	8	2	3	7
7	4	6	3	2	1	8	5	9

92

5	4	3	6	1	7	8	2	9
8	1	7	9	3	2	4	6	5
6	9	2	8	5	4	7	3	1
9	5	1	2	4	3	6	7	8
4	3	8	5	7	6	1	9	2
2	7	6	1	9	8	3	5	4
3	2	9	7	8	1	5	4	6
1	6	4	3	2	5	9	8	7
7	8	5	4	6	9	2	1	3

93

7	2	8	1	3	6	5	9	4
3	9	5	4	7	2	8	1	6
1	6	4	5	8	9	7	2	3
2	5	9	6	4	3	1	8	7
8	3	7	9	5	1	6	4	2
6	4	1	8	2	7	9	3	5
4	7	6	3	1	8	2	5	9
5	8	2	7	9	4	3	6	1
9	1	3	2	6	5	4	7	8

94

4	2	9	5	7	8	3	6	1
8	5	1	2	3	6	4	9	7
6	3	7	9	1	4	8	2	5
5	4	6	7	9	3	2	1	8
1	8	3	6	2	5	7	4	9
7	9	2	4	8	1	6	5	3
9	7	5	8	4	2	1	3	6
3	6	4	1	5	7	9	8	2
2	1	8	3	6	9	5	7	4

95

6	5	3	1	2	7	8	9	4
2	8	7	5	4	9	6	3	1
4	1	9	6	3	8	2	5	7
1	2	5	3	9	6	7	4	8
8	9	4	2	7	5	3	1	6
3	7	6	8	1	4	9	2	5
9	4	8	7	5	2	1	6	3
7	3	2	4	6	1	5	8	9
5	6	1	9	8	3	4	7	2

96

7	5	2	8	3	4	6	9	1
3	1	4	5	6	9	7	2	8
9	6	8	2	7	1	4	5	3
2	4	7	6	8	5	1	3	9
5	3	9	4	1	7	8	6	2
1	8	6	9	2	3	5	4	7
6	7	5	1	9	2	3	8	4
4	9	1	3	5	8	2	7	6
8	2	3	7	4	6	9	1	5

97

7	5	6	2	4	1	3	9	8
4	9	8	3	6	5	7	2	1
2	1	3	8	9	7	4	5	6
6	2	4	5	7	8	1	3	9
9	7	1	6	3	4	5	8	2
8	3	5	9	1	2	6	7	4
1	4	2	7	8	3	9	6	5
3	8	9	1	5	6	2	4	7
5	6	7	4	2	9	8	1	3

98

7	1	5	4	9	3	2	8	6
4	6	9	5	8	2	3	1	7
2	3	8	7	1	6	9	5	4
6	7	4	2	5	1	8	9	3
8	2	1	3	6	9	7	4	5
5	9	3	8	4	7	1	6	2
3	5	6	9	2	8	4	7	1
1	8	7	6	3	4	5	2	9
9	4	2	1	7	5	6	3	8

99

3	8	7	2	5	4	9	1	6
5	4	1	3	9	6	2	8	7
6	2	9	7	1	8	4	5	3
1	9	4	5	6	3	7	2	8
2	6	5	9	8	7	3	4	1
7	3	8	1	4	2	5	6	9
4	7	2	6	3	1	8	9	5
9	1	3	8	2	5	6	7	4
8	5	6	4	7	9	1	3	2

100

1	5	3	7	8	4	2	6	9
2	7	9	3	5	6	8	4	1
8	6	4	9	2	1	5	7	3
5	4	8	1	3	2	6	9	7
7	9	1	8	6	5	4	3	2
3	2	6	4	9	7	1	5	8
6	1	5	2	7	3	9	8	4
9	3	2	6	4	8	7	1	5
4	8	7	5	1	9	3	2	6

101

4	2	3	1	8	9	6	5	7
9	5	7	3	6	4	1	2	8
1	6	8	2	5	7	9	4	3
2	4	6	5	1	3	7	8	9
7	1	9	4	2	8	5	3	6
3	8	5	9	7	6	2	1	4
5	9	4	7	3	2	8	6	1
8	7	1	6	4	5	3	9	2
6	3	2	8	9	1	4	7	5

102

9	8	4	7	2	3	1	5	6
1	5	2	8	4	6	9	3	7
7	3	6	9	5	1	8	4	2
2	4	8	6	3	9	5	7	1
3	9	7	2	1	5	4	6	8
5	6	1	4	7	8	3	2	9
8	2	9	5	6	4	7	1	3
4	7	3	1	9	2	6	8	5
6	1	5	3	8	7	2	9	4

103

6	1	2	3	9	8	4	5	7
9	8	7	2	4	5	6	3	1
5	3	4	6	1	7	8	9	2
8	7	9	4	6	3	2	1	5
3	4	5	8	2	1	7	6	9
2	6	1	5	7	9	3	8	4
4	2	8	1	5	6	9	7	3
1	9	3	7	8	4	5	2	6
7	5	6	9	3	2	1	4	8

104

9	5	1	6	3	4	2	7	8
3	4	8	1	2	7	6	5	9
2	6	7	9	8	5	1	4	3
1	3	4	5	6	8	9	2	7
6	7	2	3	4	9	5	8	1
8	9	5	2	7	1	3	6	4
4	1	6	7	5	3	8	9	2
7	2	3	8	9	6	4	1	5
5	8	9	4	1	2	7	3	6

105

4	7	6	5	8	1	3	2	9
5	2	9	4	3	6	1	8	7
3	1	8	9	2	7	6	4	5
6	5	3	1	9	8	2	7	4
1	4	2	6	7	5	8	9	3
9	8	7	2	4	3	5	1	6
8	6	5	7	1	4	9	3	2
7	9	1	3	5	2	4	6	8
2	3	4	8	6	9	7	5	1

106

3	6	4	2	1	8	5	9	7
7	2	8	6	9	5	1	3	4
1	5	9	7	3	4	8	6	2
2	1	5	9	6	7	3	4	8
8	3	6	1	4	2	9	7	5
4	9	7	5	8	3	2	1	6
9	8	1	4	2	6	7	5	3
6	7	3	8	5	9	4	2	1
5	4	2	3	7	1	6	8	9

107

7	6	8	2	3	5	4	1	9
5	3	9	6	4	1	7	8	2
2	1	4	7	9	8	6	3	5
4	5	7	3	2	6	8	9	1
9	8	1	4	5	7	2	6	3
3	2	6	8	1	9	5	7	4
6	9	3	5	7	2	1	4	8
8	4	2	1	6	3	9	5	7
1	7	5	9	8	4	3	2	6

108

5	3	1	8	4	9	6	2	7
2	8	6	1	7	5	4	9	3
7	4	9	6	3	2	1	5	8
4	2	7	5	9	1	3	8	6
1	5	3	7	8	6	9	4	2
9	6	8	3	2	4	7	1	5
6	9	4	2	5	7	8	3	1
3	7	2	9	1	8	5	6	4
8	1	5	4	6	3	2	7	9

109

2	3	1	6	7	8	9	5	4
4	7	8	2	5	9	1	6	3
9	6	5	1	3	4	7	8	2
6	8	2	4	1	7	3	9	5
1	9	3	8	6	5	4	2	7
7	5	4	3	9	2	6	1	8
5	1	9	7	8	3	2	4	6
8	4	7	9	2	6	5	3	1
3	2	6	5	4	1	8	7	9

110

7	9	6	5	4	3	2	8	1
2	1	8	6	7	9	3	5	4
5	4	3	2	1	8	9	7	6
8	5	2	1	3	7	6	4	9
3	6	9	8	5	4	1	2	7
1	7	4	9	6	2	5	3	8
9	3	1	7	8	5	4	6	2
6	8	5	4	2	1	7	9	3
4	2	7	3	9	6	8	1	5

111

4	6	7	3	9	5	8	2	1
1	5	8	6	7	2	9	4	3
3	9	2	1	4	8	6	7	5
9	8	3	5	6	7	2	1	4
6	2	4	9	3	1	5	8	7
5	7	1	8	2	4	3	9	6
8	4	9	7	5	6	1	3	2
2	3	6	4	1	9	7	5	8
7	1	5	2	8	3	4	6	9

112

1	9	5	2	4	3	6	8	7
2	4	8	1	6	7	5	9	3
3	7	6	5	9	8	4	1	2
8	6	2	7	5	1	9	3	4
7	5	1	9	3	4	8	2	6
4	3	9	8	2	6	7	5	1
6	8	4	3	1	5	2	7	9
5	2	3	6	7	9	1	4	8
9	1	7	4	8	2	3	6	5

113

2	5	6	3	8	1	7	9	4
7	8	1	2	9	4	6	5	3
3	4	9	6	5	7	8	2	1
5	7	2	1	4	6	9	3	8
6	9	8	5	2	3	4	1	7
4	1	3	8	7	9	2	6	5
9	6	5	7	3	8	1	4	2
8	2	4	9	1	5	3	7	6
1	3	7	4	6	2	5	8	9

114

1	7	4	8	6	3	5	9	2
9	5	2	4	1	7	8	3	6
6	3	8	5	9	2	1	7	4
3	2	6	7	5	4	9	1	8
8	1	9	3	2	6	7	4	5
7	4	5	1	8	9	2	6	3
2	6	7	9	3	5	4	8	1
5	9	1	6	4	8	3	2	7
4	8	3	2	7	1	6	5	9

115

2	3	9	7	5	8	6	1	4
5	4	7	6	9	1	2	8	3
6	1	8	3	2	4	7	5	9
7	8	6	4	1	9	5	3	2
1	9	3	2	6	5	4	7	8
4	2	5	8	3	7	9	6	1
8	5	4	1	7	2	3	9	6
9	6	2	5	8	3	1	4	7
3	7	1	9	4	6	8	2	5

116

9	1	6	8	4	5	3	7	2
2	3	7	6	1	9	5	8	4
4	5	8	3	7	2	9	1	6
6	2	9	1	8	7	4	3	5
8	4	1	2	5	3	6	9	7
5	7	3	4	9	6	8	2	1
7	8	5	9	2	4	1	6	3
3	9	4	7	6	1	2	5	8
1	6	2	5	3	8	7	4	9

117

2	4	3	1	6	7	9	8	5
8	9	6	2	3	5	1	4	7
5	7	1	9	4	8	6	2	3
7	1	8	4	2	6	5	3	9
3	2	5	8	1	9	7	6	4
4	6	9	5	7	3	2	1	8
1	3	2	7	9	4	8	5	6
6	8	7	3	5	2	4	9	1
9	5	4	6	8	1	3	7	2

118

2	1	6	9	4	7	8	5	3
4	9	5	8	6	3	1	7	2
3	7	8	5	1	2	4	9	6
5	8	3	6	9	4	7	2	1
6	4	9	7	2	1	5	3	8
1	2	7	3	5	8	9	6	4
8	5	4	2	3	9	6	1	7
7	6	2	1	8	5	3	4	9
9	3	1	4	7	6	2	8	5

119

2	9	8	5	7	6	1	4	3
7	1	5	4	9	3	8	6	2
4	3	6	8	1	2	5	9	7
5	8	9	3	6	7	2	1	4
1	2	3	9	4	8	7	5	6
6	7	4	2	5	1	3	8	9
3	5	7	6	8	4	9	2	1
8	4	2	1	3	9	6	7	5
9	6	1	7	2	5	4	3	8

120

4	8	3	7	2	6	9	1	5
6	5	9	1	3	8	7	4	2
1	7	2	9	5	4	6	8	3
5	9	7	8	1	3	4	2	6
3	2	4	5	6	7	1	9	8
8	1	6	2	4	9	3	5	7
9	6	5	3	8	1	2	7	4
2	4	1	6	7	5	8	3	9
7	3	8	4	9	2	5	6	1

121

2	9	8	7	3	1	5	6	4
1	7	3	5	4	6	8	9	2
4	6	5	9	8	2	1	3	7
9	5	7	1	6	8	2	4	3
3	4	6	2	7	5	9	1	8
8	2	1	4	9	3	7	5	6
6	8	9	3	1	7	4	2	5
7	1	2	6	5	4	3	8	9
5	3	4	8	2	9	6	7	1

122

9	7	6	4	1	2	5	3	8
8	4	1	7	5	3	6	2	9
2	5	3	9	6	8	1	7	4
4	3	5	1	8	6	2	9	7
6	9	8	3	2	7	4	5	1
1	2	7	5	9	4	3	8	6
5	8	2	6	4	9	7	1	3
7	6	9	2	3	1	8	4	5
3	1	4	8	7	5	9	6	2

123

7	6	4	1	3	5	8	9	2
2	5	3	9	7	8	1	6	4
1	9	8	6	4	2	5	7	3
4	1	9	3	2	7	6	8	5
5	7	2	8	1	6	3	4	9
8	3	6	4	5	9	2	1	7
3	8	5	7	9	1	4	2	6
6	2	7	5	8	4	9	3	1
9	4	1	2	6	3	7	5	8

124

7	4	6	1	3	5	2	9	8
5	2	1	8	6	9	3	4	7
9	3	8	2	4	7	6	5	1
3	1	2	7	5	8	9	6	4
4	5	9	6	2	1	7	8	3
6	8	7	4	9	3	5	1	2
1	9	3	5	8	2	4	7	6
8	6	5	3	7	4	1	2	9
2	7	4	9	1	6	8	3	5

125

2	7	9	8	6	5	3	1	4
3	5	4	9	7	1	8	2	6
6	1	8	3	2	4	9	7	5
4	9	6	7	1	2	5	3	8
8	3	7	5	4	9	2	6	1
5	2	1	6	8	3	4	9	7
9	8	5	1	3	7	6	4	2
1	4	3	2	5	6	7	8	9
7	6	2	4	9	8	1	5	3

126

6	9	3	5	1	2	4	8	7
2	4	1	8	9	7	6	3	5
7	5	8	6	4	3	1	9	2
9	6	5	4	8	1	7	2	3
3	7	4	2	6	9	8	5	1
8	1	2	3	7	5	9	4	6
4	3	6	1	2	8	5	7	9
5	8	9	7	3	6	2	1	4
1	2	7	9	5	4	3	6	8

127

2	5	7	4	3	6	9	8	1
1	9	8	5	2	7	6	3	4
4	3	6	9	8	1	2	5	7
7	1	3	2	6	9	5	4	8
5	6	9	3	4	8	1	7	2
8	4	2	1	7	5	3	9	6
9	7	5	8	1	2	4	6	3
3	8	1	6	9	4	7	2	5
6	2	4	7	5	3	8	1	9

128

1	2	3	9	7	5	4	6	8
7	4	5	2	6	8	9	1	3
6	9	8	4	1	3	2	5	7
4	5	7	1	9	2	3	8	6
3	8	1	5	4	6	7	2	9
2	6	9	3	8	7	1	4	5
8	1	6	7	2	9	5	3	4
9	3	4	6	5	1	8	7	2
5	7	2	8	3	4	6	9	1

129

7	8	9	3	5	4	2	1	6
5	1	2	8	7	6	3	9	4
4	3	6	1	2	9	5	8	7
2	7	1	6	3	8	9	4	5
3	9	4	5	1	7	6	2	8
8	6	5	9	4	2	7	3	1
6	4	8	2	9	5	1	7	3
9	5	3	7	8	1	4	6	2
1	2	7	4	6	3	8	5	9

130

3	1	9	4	6	8	5	2	7
4	2	5	9	7	3	8	1	6
6	7	8	2	1	5	4	9	3
9	4	3	7	2	1	6	5	8
7	8	2	6	5	4	9	3	1
5	6	1	3	8	9	2	7	4
2	3	4	1	9	6	7	8	5
8	9	6	5	3	7	1	4	2
1	5	7	8	4	2	3	6	9

131

3	2	9	5	8	4	6	1	7
4	6	8	1	3	7	2	9	5
5	7	1	6	9	2	8	3	4
8	3	4	2	1	9	7	5	6
7	9	6	4	5	3	1	2	8
2	1	5	8	7	6	9	4	3
6	4	7	3	2	1	5	8	9
1	5	3	9	6	8	4	7	2
9	8	2	7	4	5	3	6	1

132

7	5	8	2	9	6	4	1	3
3	9	6	7	1	4	5	2	8
2	4	1	3	5	8	6	7	9
6	7	3	1	2	9	8	5	4
8	1	9	6	4	5	7	3	2
5	2	4	8	7	3	1	9	6
1	6	7	9	8	2	3	4	5
4	8	2	5	3	1	9	6	7
9	3	5	4	6	7	2	8	1

133

5	6	1	7	9	4	3	8	2
7	2	9	8	3	1	5	4	6
3	8	4	5	2	6	7	1	9
1	4	3	6	5	9	8	2	7
6	9	7	4	8	2	1	5	3
2	5	8	1	7	3	9	6	4
4	3	2	9	1	8	6	7	5
8	7	6	3	4	5	2	9	1
9	1	5	2	6	7	4	3	8

134

6	9	3	2	1	8	5	7	4
5	7	8	9	6	4	3	1	2
4	1	2	5	3	7	6	8	9
8	3	5	7	4	9	1	2	6
7	6	4	8	2	1	9	3	5
1	2	9	3	5	6	8	4	7
9	8	6	4	7	3	2	5	1
2	4	1	6	8	5	7	9	3
3	5	7	1	9	2	4	6	8

135

9	1	7	2	3	8	5	4	6
4	8	3	5	1	6	2	7	9
6	5	2	7	9	4	3	1	8
2	7	9	3	4	1	8	6	5
8	4	1	6	5	2	7	9	3
5	3	6	8	7	9	1	2	4
3	9	5	4	2	7	6	8	1
7	6	4	1	8	3	9	5	2
1	2	8	9	6	5	4	3	7

136

5	8	6	1	7	4	2	3	9
2	1	3	8	6	9	4	5	7
4	7	9	5	2	3	8	6	1
8	2	4	9	3	1	6	7	5
1	6	7	4	5	2	9	8	3
3	9	5	7	8	6	1	4	2
7	4	8	2	1	5	3	9	6
6	5	1	3	9	8	7	2	4
9	3	2	6	4	7	5	1	8

137

9	3	2	5	8	7	4	1	6
8	6	4	1	9	3	7	5	2
5	1	7	4	6	2	3	9	8
2	5	8	3	1	6	9	7	4
6	4	3	2	7	9	1	8	5
1	7	9	8	4	5	6	2	3
7	2	1	6	3	8	5	4	9
3	9	5	7	2	4	8	6	1
4	8	6	9	5	1	2	3	7

138

6	5	1	3	2	8	9	7	4
9	3	8	4	1	7	2	5	6
7	2	4	6	5	9	3	1	8
1	7	2	5	4	3	8	6	9
5	9	6	2	8	1	4	3	7
4	8	3	7	9	6	1	2	5
3	6	9	1	7	4	5	8	2
8	1	5	9	6	2	7	4	3
2	4	7	8	3	5	6	9	1

139

2	3	8	7	6	9	5	1	4
5	7	9	8	1	4	2	3	6
1	4	6	5	3	2	9	7	8
7	1	5	3	2	6	8	4	9
3	9	2	1	4	8	7	6	5
8	6	4	9	7	5	3	2	1
6	5	1	2	8	3	4	9	7
4	8	3	6	9	7	1	5	2
9	2	7	4	5	1	6	8	3

140

5	2	3	4	6	7	9	1	8
9	6	7	3	1	8	5	2	4
1	8	4	9	5	2	6	7	3
4	7	5	6	3	9	1	8	2
6	1	2	5	8	4	3	9	7
3	9	8	2	7	1	4	5	6
2	3	9	7	4	5	8	6	1
7	4	1	8	9	6	2	3	5
8	5	6	1	2	3	7	4	9

141

7	2	3	6	9	1	5	4	8
8	1	4	3	2	5	9	7	6
9	5	6	8	4	7	3	2	1
2	8	5	4	6	9	7	1	3
1	6	9	2	7	3	8	5	4
3	4	7	5	1	8	6	9	2
5	7	8	1	3	4	2	6	9
4	9	2	7	8	6	1	3	5
6	3	1	9	5	2	4	8	7

142

2	8	3	9	4	6	1	5	7
6	4	5	8	1	7	9	2	3
1	9	7	3	2	5	8	6	4
3	5	6	4	8	9	2	7	1
7	2	9	1	6	3	5	4	8
8	1	4	5	7	2	6	3	9
9	6	1	2	3	4	7	8	5
5	3	2	7	9	8	4	1	6
4	7	8	6	5	1	3	9	2

143

1	3	7	5	9	6	2	8	4
2	4	6	8	3	1	7	9	5
5	9	8	7	2	4	3	6	1
9	6	1	2	4	5	8	3	7
8	5	3	9	1	7	6	4	2
4	7	2	3	6	8	1	5	9
6	1	5	4	7	3	9	2	8
3	2	4	1	8	9	5	7	6
7	8	9	6	5	2	4	1	3

144

5	3	6	1	4	2	8	7	9
2	4	9	7	5	8	1	6	3
7	1	8	3	9	6	2	4	5
8	5	4	9	2	1	7	3	6
6	7	2	5	3	4	9	1	8
1	9	3	6	8	7	4	5	2
9	6	7	8	1	3	5	2	4
3	2	5	4	7	9	6	8	1
4	8	1	2	6	5	3	9	7

145

7	9	5	3	1	6	4	2	8
1	6	2	5	4	8	9	7	3
8	4	3	7	2	9	6	1	5
9	1	6	2	3	7	8	5	4
5	2	4	8	6	1	7	3	9
3	7	8	4	9	5	2	6	1
2	8	1	6	5	4	3	9	7
6	5	7	9	8	3	1	4	2
4	3	9	1	7	2	5	8	6

146

7	3	8	2	6	9	1	4	5
2	9	1	4	3	5	7	6	8
4	5	6	8	7	1	9	2	3
6	2	9	1	4	8	3	5	7
8	7	4	6	5	3	2	9	1
3	1	5	7	9	2	4	8	6
9	6	7	5	1	4	8	3	2
5	4	2	3	8	7	6	1	9
1	8	3	9	2	6	5	7	4

147

6	8	1	5	9	2	4	3	7
9	3	2	8	4	7	5	1	6
7	5	4	6	1	3	2	9	8
4	6	9	7	2	1	3	8	5
3	1	8	9	6	5	7	2	4
2	7	5	3	8	4	9	6	1
1	9	3	4	7	8	6	5	2
8	4	6	2	5	9	1	7	3
5	2	7	1	3	6	8	4	9

148

6	7	8	4	3	9	1	2	5
9	4	5	2	1	7	8	3	6
2	1	3	8	5	6	4	9	7
8	9	2	7	4	5	6	1	3
5	6	7	1	2	3	9	8	4
1	3	4	6	9	8	5	7	2
3	2	6	9	8	4	7	5	1
4	5	9	3	7	1	2	6	8
7	8	1	5	6	2	3	4	9

149

2	7	8	4	3	5	9	1	6
5	9	3	2	1	6	8	7	4
6	4	1	7	9	8	3	5	2
9	6	2	5	7	4	1	8	3
8	5	4	1	6	3	7	2	9
1	3	7	8	2	9	6	4	5
4	1	9	3	5	7	2	6	8
7	8	6	9	4	2	5	3	1
3	2	5	6	8	1	4	9	7

150

5	1	3	7	2	9	4	8	6
9	4	2	1	8	6	7	3	5
7	6	8	5	4	3	2	1	9
2	3	5	8	7	4	9	6	1
1	9	4	2	6	5	8	7	3
8	7	6	3	9	1	5	4	2
6	2	7	9	1	8	3	5	4
4	5	9	6	3	7	1	2	8
3	8	1	4	5	2	6	9	7

151

9	7	6	1	3	5	4	2	8
4	1	8	7	2	9	3	6	5
3	5	2	4	8	6	1	9	7
1	8	7	2	5	3	6	4	9
2	9	5	8	6	4	7	3	1
6	4	3	9	1	7	8	5	2
8	3	9	5	4	1	2	7	6
7	6	1	3	9	2	5	8	4
5	2	4	6	7	8	9	1	3

152

8	6	9	3	5	7	2	4	1
2	5	4	1	9	6	7	8	3
7	1	3	8	4	2	9	6	5
4	2	1	6	7	3	8	5	9
9	3	8	4	1	5	6	2	7
5	7	6	9	2	8	1	3	4
3	8	7	5	6	9	4	1	2
1	9	5	2	8	4	3	7	6
6	4	2	7	3	1	5	9	8

153

6	7	2	1	8	4	9	5	3
8	4	1	3	5	9	6	2	7
5	9	3	6	7	2	4	1	8
4	6	8	2	1	3	5	7	9
1	2	5	7	9	6	8	3	4
9	3	7	5	4	8	2	6	1
2	5	9	8	3	7	1	4	6
3	1	4	9	6	5	7	8	2
7	8	6	4	2	1	3	9	5

154

3	9	4	5	6	2	8	1	7
7	1	5	4	9	8	6	2	3
6	2	8	7	3	1	4	5	9
4	3	7	2	5	9	1	8	6
8	5	2	3	1	6	7	9	4
9	6	1	8	4	7	5	3	2
5	8	9	6	7	3	2	4	1
2	7	3	1	8	4	9	6	5
1	4	6	9	2	5	3	7	8

155

3	9	7	4	8	1	6	5	2
6	1	5	7	9	2	3	4	8
8	2	4	3	6	5	9	7	1
9	4	3	6	1	8	5	2	7
2	8	1	9	5	7	4	3	6
5	7	6	2	4	3	8	1	9
4	3	8	1	2	6	7	9	5
7	6	2	5	3	9	1	8	4
1	5	9	8	7	4	2	6	3

156

5	9	7	8	4	2	3	1	6
3	4	2	5	1	6	7	9	8
6	1	8	7	9	3	4	2	5
9	8	3	1	5	7	6	4	2
7	5	4	6	2	8	1	3	9
1	2	6	9	3	4	5	8	7
2	6	9	4	7	1	8	5	3
4	7	5	3	8	9	2	6	1
8	3	1	2	6	5	9	7	4

157

2	1	8	3	6	7	9	5	4
5	6	7	4	9	1	3	2	8
9	3	4	2	5	8	7	1	6
8	7	5	6	3	2	1	4	9
3	4	9	7	1	5	6	8	2
1	2	6	8	4	9	5	3	7
7	5	3	9	8	4	2	6	1
6	8	2	1	7	3	4	9	5
4	9	1	5	2	6	8	7	3

158

5	3	2	8	9	1	6	4	7
4	9	7	3	5	6	2	1	8
6	8	1	2	4	7	9	5	3
2	7	3	4	6	5	8	9	1
8	5	4	9	1	2	7	3	6
1	6	9	7	8	3	4	2	5
3	2	5	6	7	9	1	8	4
7	1	8	5	2	4	3	6	9
9	4	6	1	3	8	5	7	2

159

5	7	4	2	9	8	3	6	1
9	1	3	7	5	6	8	4	2
6	8	2	4	1	3	9	5	7
1	5	6	3	8	2	4	7	9
8	4	9	1	6	7	5	2	3
3	2	7	9	4	5	1	8	6
7	9	5	8	2	1	6	3	4
2	6	1	5	3	4	7	9	8
4	3	8	6	7	9	2	1	5

160

2	9	3	5	4	6	7	8	1
4	7	1	2	3	8	9	5	6
8	5	6	9	1	7	3	4	2
5	2	7	8	9	1	4	6	3
3	4	8	6	7	2	1	9	5
6	1	9	4	5	3	2	7	8
1	3	5	7	8	4	6	2	9
9	6	4	3	2	5	8	1	7
7	8	2	1	6	9	5	3	4

161

1	6	4	3	2	8	9	7	5
5	9	3	1	7	4	2	8	6
2	7	8	9	5	6	4	3	1
7	3	2	4	8	1	6	5	9
9	4	1	7	6	5	3	2	8
8	5	6	2	9	3	7	1	4
4	8	5	6	3	2	1	9	7
6	2	9	8	1	7	5	4	3
3	1	7	5	4	9	8	6	2

162

8	1	3	2	6	9	5	7	4
4	9	6	7	3	5	1	8	2
5	2	7	4	8	1	3	9	6
7	5	2	9	4	8	6	1	3
1	3	8	5	2	6	9	4	7
9	6	4	3	1	7	2	5	8
6	8	9	1	7	2	4	3	5
2	4	1	8	5	3	7	6	9
3	7	5	6	9	4	8	2	1

163

9	1	7	8	4	2	6	3	5
4	3	2	9	5	6	7	8	1
6	5	8	7	3	1	4	9	2
1	7	5	4	8	3	9	2	6
3	2	4	5	6	9	8	1	7
8	9	6	1	2	7	3	5	4
2	6	9	3	1	4	5	7	8
7	8	1	6	9	5	2	4	3
5	4	3	2	7	8	1	6	9

164

5	2	1	7	8	9	4	3	6
8	7	9	4	3	6	5	2	1
4	3	6	1	2	5	7	8	9
3	8	2	9	1	4	6	7	5
7	6	4	2	5	8	9	1	3
1	9	5	6	7	3	8	4	2
6	5	7	3	4	1	2	9	8
9	4	3	8	6	2	1	5	7
2	1	8	5	9	7	3	6	4

165

2	4	9	5	3	6	8	7	1
3	7	5	2	1	8	6	9	4
8	1	6	4	9	7	5	3	2
5	9	2	3	4	1	7	6	8
6	3	7	8	2	5	1	4	9
1	8	4	7	6	9	2	5	3
9	5	1	6	8	3	4	2	7
7	2	8	9	5	4	3	1	6
4	6	3	1	7	2	9	8	5

166

1	4	9	8	5	6	3	2	7
5	2	3	4	1	7	8	6	9
7	8	6	3	9	2	1	5	4
8	3	1	6	4	5	9	7	2
2	9	5	1	7	8	4	3	6
4	6	7	9	2	3	5	1	8
6	5	8	7	3	9	2	4	1
9	1	2	5	6	4	7	8	3
3	7	4	2	8	1	6	9	5

167

1	5	4	9	7	2	3	6	8
8	9	2	5	3	6	1	7	4
3	7	6	8	1	4	2	9	5
2	1	3	7	8	9	5	4	6
7	4	5	2	6	1	8	3	9
6	8	9	3	4	5	7	1	2
9	3	7	4	5	8	6	2	1
5	2	1	6	9	7	4	8	3
4	6	8	1	2	3	9	5	7

168

5	3	1	7	8	6	4	9	2
9	8	7	5	2	4	1	6	3
2	4	6	1	3	9	8	5	7
7	2	5	6	4	8	9	3	1
4	1	3	9	7	2	6	8	5
8	6	9	3	5	1	7	2	4
6	9	2	4	1	5	3	7	8
3	5	4	8	9	7	2	1	6
1	7	8	2	6	3	5	4	9

169

8	3	2	4	6	5	7	9	1
4	5	6	9	7	1	3	8	2
7	1	9	3	2	8	6	5	4
3	8	7	5	9	4	1	2	6
2	4	5	6	1	7	8	3	9
6	9	1	8	3	2	4	7	5
1	6	8	2	5	3	9	4	7
5	7	3	1	4	9	2	6	8
9	2	4	7	8	6	5	1	3

170

8	7	2	3	1	6	4	5	9
1	6	3	5	9	4	8	2	7
4	5	9	7	2	8	3	6	1
9	2	8	4	3	1	5	7	6
3	4	7	9	6	5	2	1	8
5	1	6	8	7	2	9	3	4
6	3	1	2	4	9	7	8	5
2	8	4	1	5	7	6	9	3
7	9	5	6	8	3	1	4	2

171

4	7	9	5	3	6	2	1	8
6	5	3	2	8	1	7	9	4
1	2	8	4	7	9	5	6	3
3	6	4	9	2	8	1	7	5
2	1	7	3	5	4	9	8	6
9	8	5	1	6	7	3	4	2
8	4	2	7	1	3	6	5	9
5	9	1	6	4	2	8	3	7
7	3	6	8	9	5	4	2	1

172

3	9	4	1	6	2	7	5	8
8	7	1	3	5	4	9	2	6
5	6	2	9	8	7	1	3	4
2	3	9	7	1	8	4	6	5
4	1	8	5	2	6	3	7	9
6	5	7	4	9	3	2	8	1
1	4	3	6	7	5	8	9	2
7	2	6	8	4	9	5	1	3
9	8	5	2	3	1	6	4	7

173

2	8	6	5	9	3	7	4	1
9	5	3	7	1	4	8	6	2
1	7	4	2	6	8	5	9	3
7	6	8	3	5	1	9	2	4
4	3	2	9	7	6	1	5	8
5	9	1	4	8	2	3	7	6
8	2	7	1	4	9	6	3	5
3	1	9	6	2	5	4	8	7
6	4	5	8	3	7	2	1	9

174

8	6	4	2	9	1	7	3	5
2	1	5	8	3	7	4	9	6
3	7	9	6	4	5	1	8	2
9	5	6	3	7	4	2	1	8
1	8	3	5	2	9	6	4	7
4	2	7	1	6	8	3	5	9
5	4	2	9	1	6	8	7	3
7	3	8	4	5	2	9	6	1
6	9	1	7	8	3	5	2	4

175

6	1	5	7	9	4	3	8	2
8	3	7	6	1	2	4	5	9
2	4	9	3	5	8	6	1	7
3	9	1	2	6	7	5	4	8
5	2	4	8	3	1	7	9	6
7	6	8	5	4	9	2	3	1
9	5	3	1	2	6	8	7	4
1	7	6	4	8	3	9	2	5
4	8	2	9	7	5	1	6	3

176

2	8	5	7	9	4	1	3	6
7	1	3	5	8	6	9	4	2
6	9	4	3	2	1	5	7	8
3	6	2	4	7	9	8	5	1
4	5	9	2	1	8	3	6	7
1	7	8	6	3	5	2	9	4
8	4	1	9	6	3	7	2	5
5	3	7	8	4	2	6	1	9
9	2	6	1	5	7	4	8	3

177

4	7	8	6	2	5	1	3	9
6	5	9	7	3	1	8	2	4
1	3	2	4	8	9	6	7	5
8	6	4	1	5	7	3	9	2
2	1	7	8	9	3	4	5	6
5	9	3	2	4	6	7	1	8
7	4	5	3	6	2	9	8	1
3	2	6	9	1	8	5	4	7
9	8	1	5	7	4	2	6	3

178

6	4	5	2	9	3	7	1	8
9	1	7	4	5	8	6	2	3
2	3	8	7	1	6	9	5	4
1	9	4	8	3	2	5	6	7
3	7	2	5	6	4	8	9	1
8	5	6	9	7	1	3	4	2
7	2	3	6	4	5	1	8	9
5	8	1	3	2	9	4	7	6
4	6	9	1	8	7	2	3	5

179

4	2	3	6	9	5	7	8	1
7	6	5	8	2	1	3	9	4
8	9	1	3	7	4	2	6	5
3	5	9	4	8	6	1	7	2
2	1	7	5	3	9	6	4	8
6	8	4	7	1	2	5	3	9
1	7	2	9	6	8	4	5	3
9	4	6	1	5	3	8	2	7
5	3	8	2	4	7	9	1	6

180

5	3	1	6	7	2	9	8	4
4	7	2	5	9	8	3	1	6
9	6	8	4	1	3	7	5	2
2	9	4	8	6	1	5	3	7
6	8	7	3	2	5	4	9	1
1	5	3	7	4	9	2	6	8
3	2	9	1	8	7	6	4	5
8	4	5	2	3	6	1	7	9
7	1	6	9	5	4	8	2	3

181

9	2	7	5	6	1	8	4	3
5	6	1	3	4	8	9	7	2
3	4	8	2	9	7	5	6	1
7	9	6	4	2	3	1	8	5
1	3	4	9	8	5	6	2	7
8	5	2	7	1	6	4	3	9
6	1	3	8	7	9	2	5	4
4	8	5	1	3	2	7	9	6
2	7	9	6	5	4	3	1	8

182

5	4	2	9	3	1	7	6	8
7	1	8	6	2	4	9	3	5
6	9	3	5	8	7	1	4	2
3	5	4	2	6	9	8	7	1
1	8	9	3	7	5	4	2	6
2	6	7	4	1	8	3	5	9
8	7	5	1	4	6	2	9	3
9	3	1	7	5	2	6	8	4
4	2	6	8	9	3	5	1	7

183

8	6	5	2	4	7	1	3	9
1	2	4	6	9	3	5	7	8
7	3	9	8	1	5	6	2	4
4	8	3	1	6	2	7	9	5
9	7	2	3	5	4	8	1	6
5	1	6	7	8	9	2	4	3
6	4	8	9	2	1	3	5	7
2	9	7	5	3	8	4	6	1
3	5	1	4	7	6	9	8	2

184

1	3	2	8	9	5	7	6	4
9	4	5	3	6	7	2	1	8
7	6	8	2	4	1	5	3	9
2	1	3	7	8	6	9	4	5
8	7	4	1	5	9	3	2	6
6	5	9	4	2	3	8	7	1
4	8	6	9	3	2	1	5	7
3	9	1	5	7	4	6	8	2
5	2	7	6	1	8	4	9	3

185

2	9	5	7	8	3	6	4	1
3	6	4	2	5	1	9	7	8
7	8	1	4	9	6	5	3	2
1	3	6	9	4	7	2	8	5
4	2	9	5	1	8	7	6	3
5	7	8	6	3	2	1	9	4
8	1	2	3	6	9	4	5	7
6	4	3	1	7	5	8	2	9
9	5	7	8	2	4	3	1	6

186

9	3	7	2	8	1	4	5	6
8	6	2	5	7	4	9	1	3
4	1	5	6	3	9	8	2	7
7	8	1	9	2	5	6	3	4
5	2	6	8	4	3	1	7	9
3	9	4	7	1	6	5	8	2
1	7	9	3	6	8	2	4	5
6	4	3	1	5	2	7	9	8
2	5	8	4	9	7	3	6	1

187

6	2	9	8	1	7	4	5	3
3	1	7	2	5	4	8	9	6
5	8	4	3	9	6	7	2	1
8	4	2	5	7	3	1	6	9
1	3	6	4	8	9	2	7	5
9	7	5	6	2	1	3	8	4
2	5	1	9	4	8	6	3	7
7	6	8	1	3	5	9	4	2
4	9	3	7	6	2	5	1	8

188

7	3	4	2	6	1	5	9	8
6	1	5	4	9	8	2	3	7
2	8	9	3	5	7	6	4	1
9	7	3	5	2	4	1	8	6
1	6	8	9	7	3	4	5	2
4	5	2	1	8	6	3	7	9
5	9	1	8	4	2	7	6	3
3	4	7	6	1	9	8	2	5
8	2	6	7	3	5	9	1	4

189

1	6	8	9	3	5	2	7	4
3	2	5	6	7	4	1	9	8
7	4	9	2	1	8	5	6	3
6	5	4	7	2	3	8	1	9
2	9	3	4	8	1	7	5	6
8	1	7	5	9	6	3	4	2
4	7	6	8	5	2	9	3	1
9	3	2	1	6	7	4	8	5
5	8	1	3	4	9	6	2	7

190

2	7	4	8	1	6	9	5	3
9	8	6	5	3	4	7	2	1
5	3	1	9	2	7	8	6	4
8	5	9	1	4	2	6	3	7
3	1	7	6	8	9	2	4	5
4	6	2	7	5	3	1	9	8
1	2	3	4	9	8	5	7	6
7	4	5	2	6	1	3	8	9
6	9	8	3	7	5	4	1	2

191

1	7	8	5	2	4	6	3	9
9	6	3	7	1	8	4	2	5
5	4	2	9	6	3	1	8	7
8	1	5	3	7	9	2	4	6
4	9	7	6	8	2	3	5	1
3	2	6	1	4	5	7	9	8
6	8	4	2	9	1	5	7	3
2	5	1	8	3	7	9	6	4
7	3	9	4	5	6	8	1	2

192

5	6	2	8	3	4	7	1	9
4	1	8	7	2	9	5	3	6
9	7	3	1	5	6	2	8	4
3	9	4	2	6	8	1	7	5
8	5	1	9	4	7	6	2	3
6	2	7	5	1	3	9	4	8
7	8	5	4	9	2	3	6	1
1	4	6	3	7	5	8	9	2
2	3	9	6	8	1	4	5	7

193

9	1	4	5	2	7	3	6	8
8	5	6	9	3	1	2	7	4
7	2	3	8	6	4	9	5	1
6	3	8	1	5	2	7	4	9
1	7	9	6	4	8	5	2	3
2	4	5	7	9	3	1	8	6
5	9	2	4	1	6	8	3	7
4	8	1	3	7	5	6	9	2
3	6	7	2	8	9	4	1	5

194

4	1	8	6	3	7	5	9	2
2	6	5	4	9	1	7	8	3
9	7	3	5	2	8	4	6	1
5	8	9	3	6	4	1	2	7
6	3	2	1	7	9	8	5	4
7	4	1	2	8	5	9	3	6
3	5	4	8	1	2	6	7	9
1	9	6	7	5	3	2	4	8
8	2	7	9	4	6	3	1	5

195

9	7	4	8	5	1	2	3	6
3	1	8	4	6	2	5	9	7
6	5	2	3	7	9	1	4	8
8	3	5	9	4	6	7	1	2
4	9	7	2	1	5	8	6	3
1	2	6	7	8	3	9	5	4
7	6	3	1	9	8	4	2	5
2	8	9	5	3	4	6	7	1
5	4	1	6	2	7	3	8	9

196

6	2	5	1	3	7	4	9	8
3	1	4	5	9	8	6	2	7
7	8	9	4	2	6	1	3	5
5	7	6	9	8	3	2	1	4
4	3	1	2	6	5	7	8	9
2	9	8	7	1	4	3	5	6
8	4	2	6	5	1	9	7	3
9	6	3	8	7	2	5	4	1
1	5	7	3	4	9	8	6	2

197

5	4	8	3	2	6	7	9	1
3	2	7	8	1	9	5	6	4
6	1	9	7	5	4	3	2	8
1	7	5	2	9	3	8	4	6
4	9	3	6	7	8	2	1	5
2	8	6	1	4	5	9	7	3
9	3	2	5	6	1	4	8	7
7	5	1	4	8	2	6	3	9
8	6	4	9	3	7	1	5	2

198

3	5	6	7	4	9	2	8	1
2	8	9	5	6	1	4	7	3
4	1	7	8	3	2	9	5	6
5	3	2	6	7	8	1	9	4
7	6	1	9	5	4	3	2	8
9	4	8	1	2	3	5	6	7
6	2	4	3	8	5	7	1	9
1	7	5	4	9	6	8	3	2
8	9	3	2	1	7	6	4	5

199

4	5	7	3	1	2	8	9	6
9	6	3	5	8	4	1	7	2
2	8	1	6	7	9	3	4	5
5	4	9	2	6	1	7	8	3
7	3	6	4	5	8	2	1	9
8	1	2	7	9	3	5	6	4
1	2	5	9	4	7	6	3	8
3	7	4	8	2	6	9	5	1
6	9	8	1	3	5	4	2	7

200

3	1	2	9	8	7	4	6	5
8	4	7	2	5	6	3	9	1
5	9	6	4	3	1	8	2	7
1	5	8	6	9	3	2	7	4
9	6	4	7	2	5	1	8	3
2	7	3	1	4	8	9	5	6
6	2	1	3	7	9	5	4	8
7	8	9	5	1	4	6	3	2
4	3	5	8	6	2	7	1	9

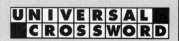